Glimpses of Gospel Life

Edited by Doriana Zamboni

Glimpses of Gospel Life

The 'Little Flowers' of Chiara
and the Focolare Movement

New City

First published as *I fioretti di Chiara e dei Focolari*
by
Edizioni San Paolo
Milan, Italy
© 2002 Edizioni San Paolo

First published in English
by
New City
Unit 17
Sovereign Park
Coronation Road
London NW10 7QP

Translated by Stella Worthington
English translation © New City, London 2004

British Cataloguing-in-Publication Data
A catalogue record for this book is available
from the British Library
ISBN 0 904287 89 0

Cover design by Tomeu Mayans
Typeset by New City Press, New York
Printed and bound by Versa Press, Peoria, Illinois

Contents

Introduction 9

The First Time 13
The Open Envelope 14
Perfect Joy. 15
The Heavily Laden Table 16
My Experience of Living the Gospel. 17
Half an Hour Away From Death 18
God's Timeliness 20
An Important Appointment. 21
An Agreement Between Two Guardian Angels . . 22
The Gift of a Large House in Paris 24
Something New 25
The Three Coats. 27
You are a Priest!. 28
The Other Mother. 29
A Lake Between the Mountains 30
Five Thousand Dollars 30
Immediately 31
The Ideal of My Life 33
For the Last Time 34
A New House 35

A Whole Ham. 36
The Exact Amount and More 37
The Geography Exam 38
Unconditional Faith. 40
All Were My Size 40
More Than Was Needed 41
The Gift of a Doll 42
Until We Meet Again in Heaven 42
Why Doubt? 43
You Are Asking Too Much of Me, Jesus. 43
The Sound Mixer Breaks Down 44
At the Time of *Solidarnosc* 45
I Am An Atheist, But You Must Be Mad 46
A Family Rebuilt 47
At the Iron Works. 48
The Courage to Uphold Your Principles. 49
From a Heart of Stone to One of Flesh 51
The Rocking Chair 52
Now You're Coming With Me 53
A Letter Containing Fifteen Thousand Francs. . . 54
So It Works!. 55
A Flower Vase. 56
Love Conquers Everything 56
An Exceptional Gift 58
It Could Have Been An Iron 60
A Well Packed Box 61
The 'Sweetener' 61
The Situation Was Turned Round 62
Fifty-Four Litres of Oil 63
Writing From Chicago 64

Excellent Marks 65
Like the Early Days 65
After Ten Minutes on the Telephone 66
A New Water Mattress 67
A Suspended Contract 68
Just Right 69
Give to Caesar What Belongs to Caesar. 70
A Special Bicycle 70
As an Inspector 71
Blessed Illness 73
The Poorest Priest 74
Private or State School 74
Your Son is Like My Son 77
Size 47 Shoes 79
The Founding of Mariapolis 'Life'. 81
Queuing Up For Water 83
A Thousand Dollars. 83
The World Will Change. 85
The Fatherhood of God 87
The Last Address 88
He Felt Love. 88
Continual Providence from God. 90
A Grace Received 92
The Hundredfold 93
A Mother Who is Beautiful Too 94
Double the Amount of Providence 96
If God Is With Us … 97
The Gospel's Revolution is Infectious 98
Algeria, the Festival of Eid 100
An E-mail from God 101

Because of an Act of Love 103
An Inspection Lasting Four Months 104
Workers for his Vineyard 105
Our Small Hall. 106
He Will Take Care of Us. 107
Landing in the Mountains in Cameroon 107
Mary's Crown 109
The Robbers' Excuses 110
They Spoke of a Miracle 112
Baby Jesus 113
Handed Back to her Mother 114
Zero Sum 115
My Yes. 116
Alive by Miracle 118
We Can Move Mountains 120

Chiara Lubich and the Focolare Movement:
   A Brief History. 121

Introduction

This book reflects a central, vital aspect of the Focolare Movement's spirituality. The Movement, which came into being as the Second World War raged, was born, so to speak, with the Gospel in its hand.

From the moment our story began, we lived the Word of God with intensity. This was our only guide and our rule of life, especially as we could not dare think about the future.

With the help of the charism that the Holy Spirit had given us, we had what you could describe as a new understanding of the Word of God. Although we had heard its words many times before, it was as if a light had been lit beneath them. And so they appeared new to us; they suited all times and were therefore eternal; they spoke to everyone and were therefore universal: made for young and old, cultured and unlearned, people of every language and nation. Our task was not only to meditate on them, but to live them and to put them into practice.

And so they re-evangelized our hearts and minds and gave new strength to our will-power.

Living the words of God, we discovered the truthfulness of the Gospel: because God keeps his promises. His response to our requests seemed as assured as a mathematical formula.

And this brought about joy at that time, as it does today, a joy that, 'no one can take away' (cf. Jn 16:22).

It has brought about love for each person and conversions to God.

Every day we have to do better, of course, because our unfaithfulness, or laziness, or tiredness hinders God's actions. But we always start again.

These glimpses of Gospel life, these 'little flowers' gathered from everyday events, are experiences of things that have actually happened to Chiara Lubich, the founder of the Focolare Movement, and to members of the Movement throughout the world.

At times they are tiny things that, nevertheless, have something extraordinary within them. They blossom into enchantment and are striking because of the light they contain. The almost child-like frankness they display is moving and makes the heart rejoice.

They teach us to see the little things of human existence as part of the weave of a divine tapestry, and so simplify life's many problems.

Above all they demonstrate that God exists, because when Christians give to him, he gives back to us; when we ask, he replies; he consoles our tears and the tears of others; he clothes us as he does the lilies of the field; we are without everything and he fills us with good things; we ask for the impossible and we receive it; we cast our worries upon him and he sorts them out one by one; he thinks far more of us than of the sparrows; we call him and there he is at our side; we have more faith in him than in anything else in the world, and he is present in all the circumstances of our life.

He is there always, unfailingly. He may intervene straight away or after some time. But he always does.

The huge number of 'little flowers' that have been gathered in preparing this book almost cry out. They are further proof, among other things, that the new currents of life within the Church, that is, Movements such as the Focolare, are a return to the radicality of the Gospel.

And from our heart endless thanks to God pour out for what he does. When someone is simple of heart and poor, that person is more his, more utterly pervaded by the Gospel.

We tell these stories to give glory to God and, we hope, to give light and courage to many.

Doriana Zamboni

The First Time

It was during 1943.

The Focolare Movement was just beginning in Trent and the war was raging. We, the first focolarine,[1] could take only a small New Testament into the air-raid shelter, which we read and put into practice word by word throughout the day. We were struck particularly by the words of Jesus which say that whatever we do to our neighbour, good or bad, will be considered done to him: 'You have done it to me' (Mt 25:40).

Now, one day Chiara[2] met a poor man in the street who said to her, 'Give me a pair of shoes, size 42.'

How could we find a pair of shoes, during the war, when there was nothing to be had. Furthermore, such a specific size: 42? She could see a little church. She went inside. It was empty, but the red light assured her that Jesus was there.

'Jesus,' she asked him kneeling down in front of the tabernacle, 'give me a pair of size 42 shoes for you in that man in need.'

She was about to leave. The door opened and she saw a girl she knew, who put a parcel into her hands. 'For the poor people you're in touch with,' she said.

---

1. Focolarine are women who live in a focolare centre, a community of the Focolare Movement. These centres are also called simply 'focolares'. The singular form for a woman who lives in a focolare is focolarina. The men are called focolarini, singular form: focolarino.
2. Each time the name Chiara is mentioned in this book, it refers to Chiara Lubich, founder and president of the Focolare Movement, who is known everywhere by her first name.

Chiara removed the paper: a pair of shoes size 42!

'So Jesus' promises are true!' The joy in her heart was immense. Jesus is still alive today after two thousand years!

This was, perhaps, the first event that showed it to us. This book offers a taste.

D.Z. – Rocca di Papa (Rome)

The Open Envelope

It was while we were still in the first focolare in Trent.

One morning Chiara was preparing lunch when the doorbell rang. It was a poor woman who asked for some help for her family. Chiara went to a drawer and took out an envelope, which contained money to pay the rent, gas and electricity for the month. She gave it all to the woman. Then she said to Jesus, 'I'll leave open the envelope, you see what to do to fill it so that we can pay what we have to.' And she began to work again.

Soon after, Natalia came rushing up on her bicycle. She had left the office during a break, and almost out of breath, she said to Chiara, 'I had a pay rise this morning and I thought I'd bring it straight away, because you might need it.'

It was double what Chiara had given.

D. Z. – Rome

Perfect Joy

Chiara and Marilen, one of Chiara's first companions, went from Trent to Rovigo, to visit some people whose addresses they had, in order to continue to deepen their understanding of our Ideal.[3] After they had walked for a long time, evening was approaching and they were making their way towards a convent where they were to be given hospitality for the night in the sisters' parlour.

Because they were later than expected, Marilen decided to go and pick up a suitcase which had been left with a priest that morning. In the meantime, night fell. On her return she rang the bell to the main door to the convent for some time, but no one came to answer it.

Next to her, squatting on the doorstep was a poor man hunched up out of the rain. She tried ringing again. It seemed as though someone was whispering, but … nothing. Knowing that Chiara was inside, wet through and not having had supper, Marilen began to be concerned.

After a little while she saw Chiara, smiling and happy, coming towards her from the back of the convent, carrying her long-handled straw bag. She took Marilen under her arm and explained, 'They saw you from the window and said you were with a young man. They thought we were girls of ill repute. They came to me and told me to leave because there wasn't anywhere for us to sleep.'

---

3. The word 'Ideal' stands for the spirituality of unity'.

Marilen replied, 'They sent us away? But it was a poor man!'

And Chiara walking and jumping with joy said, 'We're living the life of Jesus, he too was sent away.'

Marilen couldn't help but share her happiness.

Not having the money for a hotel, they decided to go to someone they knew, a non-believer. He gave them his comfortable slippers to wear, a drink to revive them and sent his children to sleep at their grandmother's so that they could have the room. Everything was done in an orderly and gentlemanly manner.

As soon as they went to bed Chiara became thoughtful. Marilen looked at her, 'You see,' said Chiara, 'quite naturally we went to bring our ideal to people who are religious, to the good, because we think that they will understand it more. But maybe it's made more for others. Perhaps God wants us to go and search for those who are far from him.'

So having experienced that 'perfect joy', it became clear to Chiara that one of the main aims of the Movement would be for us to dedicate ourselves to those who resemble Jesus crucified and forsaken, the figure of all those who, for whatever reason, are far from God.

M.H.- Trent

The Heavily Laden Table

It must have been one day in 1949. Marilen wrote about it:

I remember that walk uphill in the dark to reach the church. Those who came to be known as the first focolarine would come from outside town. Valeria and her sister Angelella would come running. Once they came without wearing their shoes, as their parents tried everything to keep them at home. But the 'call'[4] within in each one's heart was too strong. They did all they could so that they could be there. After the mass we stayed for a long time having breakfast together. It was the only time we could be with one another. At eight o'clock we would leave. We had to go to work and in the evening there were many people to attend to, particularly the poor.

One morning, climbing the steps leading to the Church, Chiara commented, 'We haven't any money at all, not even for breakfast. But Jesus is our spouse, he'll take care of it.'

Returning home from the church we found the table heavily laden with food: next to the cups, a jug of milk, some sweet bread with sultanas and a packet of cocoa.

It was only later that we realized an elderly woman, one of our neighbours, had wanted to give us a surprise. After all, the key was still hanging from the doorframe!

M.H. - Trent

My Experience of Living the Gospel

Having decided to answer God's call and give him everything, I felt it was right to give away what I didn't need, including my clothing.

Tidying up what I had left, I realized that I no longer had a silk scarf, which would have been useful to me.

---

4. The call to live the spirit of unity.

What's more, I couldn't find a pair of winter socks which I used to wear inside my boots. But what did it matter? I was happy and felt free having kept only what I needed!

That evening my sister, who knew nothing about this, said to me, 'Do you know, at work for my birthday, I was given a beautiful silk scarf and now I have two. Do you need one perhaps?'

I was amazed, that scarf seemed to have rained down from heaven.

The next day, my brother said laughing, 'I don't know how I did it. The other day I bought some socks but I can't get into them because they are too small. I'll buy some new ones. By any chance do you need them?'

I felt a lump in my throat, I was so moved. They were little things, but they seemed beautiful. I discovered that the words of the Gospel are true.

D.C. - (France)

Half an Hour Away From Death

On 1 November 1960, having finished dinner and cleared up the kitchen, I left the focolare house to buy what was needed to make a hot wine drink for a focolarino who had a cold.

I was on foot, approximately 50 metres from the gate at Villa Maria Assunta, our centre, when I was knocked down by a car. I was catapulted into the air and then into a ditch. The driver was unable to lift me into his car, because I had fainted and was a little too heavy and no one passing by stopped to give a hand.

After an hour I was able to get up on my own. The driver who had hit me, offering to help me into his car, asked, 'Shall I take you to the hospital?'

'No, to Villa Assunta,' I replied.

Leaving the car I went into one of the rooms and told my friends that I had been hurt.

Enzo took me to the hospital in Marino where for three days I was on the point of death.

On the third day, I became paralysed down my left side and one eye was bulging because of a build up of blood. I was given the anointing of the sick and the hospital administrator advised Chiara that nothing more could be done for me: it was the end.

Chiara did not give up. Everything possible had to be done to save the life of a focolarino. She prayed and asked others to do the same during the night. Then, having learned that there was a specialist in a certain type of operation that was very rare at that time, she sent for him straight away. He came and, with the inadequate equipment there at the hospital, attempted the operation. It was a question of drilling a hole in my skull to drain the blood. He did it so well that as soon as he had finished I came immediately back to life.

The next morning a thanksgiving mass was celebrated. But I know that if God had not intervened I would have died that All Saints Day in 1960, because the consultant who performed the operation told me, 'I operated on you when you were a half hour from death: you already had the death rattle.'

And so I have continued to work for the Movement, at first in Italy, then for twenty-five years in Africa and later in Madagascar for five years.

V.B. - Rocca di Papa (Rome).

God's Timeliness

It was the end of the month and there wasn't much money in the focolare in Rome to feed six people. We had just finished lunch when there was a knock on the door.

On answering it there was a gypsy, a friend of ours, who was carrying a small child.

She often came to us and we would always give her something to take away as well as some money to send to her family. But what was I to do that day? Send her away with nothing?

My first thought was: I simply can't help. I, too, had hardly any food for my friends who were my nearest neighbours!

I was just about to say I was sorry… but the words died in my mouth. In my heart I remembered, 'I was hungry and you gave me to eat.'

I smiled at the woman and asked her to come and sit down and I set a place at the table for herself and her child. I gave her what little soup was left, which I was about to increase by adding water and a stock cube, for supper. I picked up the only remaining egg and a little rice for her to take home: that was all. And in my heart I felt peace and joy.

The gypsy left the table happy, she had eaten today. I walked with her smiling to the door. She stopped and said to me, ' I don't have the money to get home.' I gave her half of what money I had, enough for a tram ticket.

At 10 o'clock that night, I was home alone preparing for an exam and the others had gone to a community meeting.

There was a knock at the door. My first reaction was don't answer, I have to study!

But then I thought maybe someone is in difficulty. Perhaps they need help.

I opened the door. It was the grocer's assistant from the shop below with a huge box of groceries. He said to me, 'Mrs P. (the mother of one of my friends in the house) has paid me to deliver these items every month. I had a bit of time today, so I put the order together and I've come. Please excuse the lateness.'

I opened the box and there was everything, from oil to wine, pasta to eggs, butter, cheese, coffee... and in abundance!

I was spellbound by God's timeliness.

D.F. - Italy

An Important Appointment

I had an important appointment to do with my spiritual life, and it meant a lot to me. Coming back from town, I barely had time to catch the bus.

I used the journey to say the rosary in silence. I asked Mary to help me spend the time well, so that I would be prepared spiritually when I arrived. After a few kilometres I realized, with concern, that the bus was not taking the normal route. Overcoming the inevitable agitation I decided to put myself completely into the hands of God, who is love.

On arrival at the terminus I went to ask some information of the driver. What he said was far from encouraging. It was then that I remembered the Word of Life, which had really struck me that month, 'Whoever does not leave father and mother ... and even his own life, cannot be my disciple.' (Lk 14:26)

Yes, if that is what God wants, I can postpone this very important meeting. And I began to love my neighbour, who at that moment was the driver. Before parking, while I was preparing to get off the bus, he said to me, 'But where do you want to go?'

'To the Focolare Centre,' I replied.

'Stay in your seat. I'll take you,' he replied.

On the way I heard that three months earlier he had met the focolarini, and from them he too had learned how to love more. Delighted, I arrived at my destination... by bus and still in time.

M. P. – Seminarian – Philippines

An Agreement Between Two Guardian Angels

It was a beautiful spring day, full of light and I was drawn to contemplate creation and God's love.

I was cycling down the winding round towards Piantonia (the road from Berceto going towards Fornovo di Parma) all the time thinking of Jesus in the Eucharist who I was carrying with me and somewhat heedless of the danger that a bicycle on one bend or another might hurtle off the road.

A sick man I had visited the day before was waiting for Holy Communion. I quite often leave the confines of the parish to exercise my ministry. But that day it wasn't me leading the excursion.

At a certain point, to my amazement, I found myself in a village in the middle of nowhere and almost automatically stopped, 'Where am I? What's happening? How come I've missed the road when I know it so well?'

I looked round almost to reassure myself that I wasn't dreaming and noticed a rather rustic looking farmhouse, and in front of me was a door which then opened.

A woman in tears appeared, and she looked at me with incredulous eyes.

She took in what she saw and cried out with happiness despite the tears, 'A priest, a priest! My Angel, thank you for answering my prayer and sending him to me!'

She approached me and said, 'Please come in, Father, my husband is on the point of death and has just asked if he could see a priest. I was desperate and being on my own I couldn't leave him and I didn't even know where to go to find a priest. It had always been my wish, though he had always refused, that he should want a priest at this moment. I turned to my guardian angel that he should find one. I have been praying intensely in expectation.

'And now here's a priest, as if sent straight from heaven. Thank you, Father, thank you. Please come in.'

And I realized that in that last half hour, that lady's guardian angel, in agreement with mine, had led me, without me even realizing, where the most urgent need for my ministry lay.

The meeting with the sick man, although in the final moments of his life on earth, was a paradise, a paradise of mercy and of love, a celebration which had been poured out on us, almost rapt in an ecstasy of wonder and of gratitude.

Yet another surprise awaited me. While I was taking the host out of the pyx to give it to the sick man, I realized with astonishment that it contained two hosts, whereas I was certain I had put only one inside. I remained in adoration beside the dying man, and a few moments later he left for heaven.

I continued my journey towards the house of the sick person I had first intended to visit.

When I arrived, his family asked, 'Why are you so late, Father, you are normally so punctual?' I explained to them why it was. Taken aback and full of fervour, they made a sincere decision. 'You know, Father, listening to your story makes us want to come to church next Sunday, so that we too can have the opportunity to go to confession and receive Holy Communion.' They were the father, mother, brother and sister of the sick man, and had not been to church for some time.

In the following days I sensed the presence of my guardian angel far more than I had done before, smiling and perhaps gently cautioning me, repeating: 'Never forget me. I will be with you always.'

A.B. – Frascati (Rome)

The Gift of a Large House in Paris

It was in 1970. The Movement had been in France since 1950.

The words of Jesus, 'May they all be one,' were and still are meant for us. Supernatural love spreads by itself and has formed a family, even in this nation, one that grows more and more numerous.

'But where can we meet?' we asked ourselves.

In October, together with Chiara, we put together a prayer to the Father in the following terms: 'If this is what you want, give us somewhere that will be like the heart of the Movement in France.'

Two months later, on New Year's Eve, the telephone rang.

A woman wanted an appointment and she explained why with a question, 'I am looking for a Movement that is apostolic and ecumenical and that loves Mary. I have heard of you. Would you be interested in a large house and two halls to meet in?'

After four years of checking everything out, the woman said to us, 'Yes, now I know that it was the Holy Spirit who guided me to choose your Movement. I am grateful to God. It's a response from heaven for me.'

It was 14 December 1974.

Chiara came to Paris for the completion, and, in the presence of the bishop and the family of the whole of the Movement, accepted the gift of the house in the middle of Paris, which we had asked of the Father in October 1970.

D.B. - France

Something New

I was born into a rich family. It was enough for me to say that I liked something and immediately my parents bought it for me. I had toys, books, lots of shoes…

Every day it was the same routine. I would put on a nice dress, go to a good school, go horse riding, learn English, but inside I felt a sense of emptiness.

When I was twelve, a friend gave me a copy of the Gospel. I read it in one go. The life Jesus proposed to the first Christians attracted me and I felt I wanted to be like them.

I told my parents that I wanted to be christened. At that time I knew some young people who belonged to the Movement.

I found them to be people who lived the Gospel in a radical way. I wanted to live like that. I raced home, opened my wardrobe and took out my most beautiful dresses to parcel up and take to the poor. For the first time I felt a great joy in my heart.

For a family such as mine, used to having things and buying things, giving things away was strange. My mother didn't understand me, but she was the first one I wanted to start to love.

She didn't like cooking, so we often ate out at restaurants. It was an unnecessary waste of money and I decided to learn how to cook to make meals which everyone liked. I wasn't always successful and sometimes I burned the supper, but the desire to love my parents was greater than ever.

One day our maid fell ill, and so there was a further opportunity within the family to love. I learned how to brush the floors, to clean, to tidy the house and above all to iron: there were tons of clothes to iron!

A few months later something began to stir in my mother: she opened the wardrobe to look for things she could give away.

One day our shop assistant's drug-dependent son took a turn for the worse. His mother, desperate, asked for my mother's help. Usually my mother would have made a decision on her own. Instead, this time she rang me so that we could see together what to do. We decided that the assistant should stay at home to look after her son and I would do her work. Throughout those months my parents rang the woman each day to ask about her son and to see if there was something that they could do.

And so, little by little, love has penetrated our family and it has become an everyday reality.

I now think that giving and loving, with inevitable highs and lows, have taken the place of a culture of having and possessing.

Q. - Lisbon

The Three Coats

All three of my small children needed winter coats, but we didn't have enough money.

That morning a big sale was advertised in the newspaper.

I would have to rush to catch the bargains. But a short time later, my sister-in-law telephoned to ask if she could come round. This didn't happen very often and so I said yes. I decided to risk losing the opportunity to save some money to be able to love Jesus in her.

When my sister-in-law arrived, she was carrying a big bag containing three coats, one for each of the children.

M.B. - New York

You are a Priest!

I was walking along the road in Manila. A youth approached me and when he was a short distance away he unsheathed a knife and pointed it at me: 'Give me all your money!' he demanded.

'Certainly,' I replied, 'and I think that you are hungry too. Look, there's a restaurant here, come and eat and drink what you want.' He was taken aback a little, but he followed me. He ate and drank until he'd had enough and I asked with love about his family. He told me he needed everything: food, clothes, shoes... I promised him that the next day I'd prepare a box of clothing for him and I gave him my address. He left in better spirits.

The next day he arrived, hesitant, ready to run, fearing a trap. He took the parcel and said to me, 'My neighbour is as poor as me and needs some help.' I invited him to return the next day to collect some things for his friend.

He came back and looked at me. I smiled at him and offered him the new parcel.

I was happy because I was giving food and clothing to Jesus in him.

He threw himself on to his knees and shaking, exclaimed, 'You are a priest, listen to my confession.'

I listened and he left happy.

From that time, he, his family and his friend's family come to our community meetings.[5]

G.M. - Philippines

---

5. Meetings locally of the Focolare Movement.

The Other Mother

A young woman, in a state of great excitement, came to the hospital for an examination. It was for a pregnancy test and, in a rather arrogant manner, she explained that she needed it straight away because she wanted an abortion.

Over and above what she said, and her outward appearance, I realized she was confused and in difficulties, so much so, that at that moment she couldn't see any other solution to her problems than an abortion.

I don't remember what I said to her, I know that I loved her and listened to her, trying to absorb her bewilderment like a sponge. She stayed with me for a long time and then she left more calmly, without saying a word.

After some months she reappeared in the clinic. She greeted me and asked if I remembered her. I replied that I did, but I didn't dare ask her what decision she had made.

She took me by the hand quite forcefully, and asked me to follow her. Outside, in the corridor, there was a baby carriage. She lifted up the cover, which was all lace and flowers, and turned towards me.

'Doctor, this is my daughter. The last time I came here I was desperate and wanted an abortion. You listened to me and I was able to think it through. I thought about it all that night and now, here she is.'

Then she turned towards the little girl, 'See? This is your other mother.'

E.S. – Italy

A Lake Between the Mountains

As part of our job we had to transport some merchandise by van. It was possible to take one of two routes: one was restful and panoramic and ran near some lakes. This one appealed to us whereas the motorway was more direct and quicker, but undoubtedly more boring.

We needed to get there by a specific time, and as there was a lot of work to do, we needed to be quick.

Happy to do God's will, even in these circumstances, we took the quicker route.

To our surprise, half way through the journey we saw a beautiful little lake between the mountains. It was shining and reflected the marvellous colours of nature. There was a sign close by with written, 'Lake Providence'.

How tender God's love is!

D.P. - Loppiano (Florence)

Five Thousand Dollars

At the hospital in Fontem,[6] Cameroon, to be able to reach the people who are very poor who come for treatment, we try to keep the cost of prescriptions and medicines very low. Even the doctors and nurses, who come from Europe, do not receive a proper salary, just an allowance for their keep.

Some time around 1980, for month after month, the number of sick people who came for treatment at the

---

6. Little town of the focolarini in Africa.

hospital grew less, because during the dry season people were more concerned with making sure that there was enough food for the whole year. This meant that the hospital's small income was further reduced. After a few months, the little that had been set aside for unforeseen problems had been used, and there was no longer any money to buy medicines or pay the salary of the locally hired staff.

We, the doctors and nurses, met together to decide what to do and to see whether to increase the prices for treatment and for medicines, but at the end of the meeting it was decided unanimously not to increase the prices or ask for extra money from the patients, rather we would trust in God, entrusting ourselves to his care.

And so, every day, together with the hospital staff, we asked God, in the name of Jesus, for providence for the hospital.

On the 31st of that month the answer came. Five thousand dollars from an anonymous donor arrived in the hospital's bank account. This covered the deficit of the previous months and staff salaries. From that day more sick people came to the hospital and there was no longer a lack of funds.

A.P.M. - Rome

Immediately

We were a group of six young men who lived in Milan in a small apartment. We lived together to prepare ourselves for what we had discovered was our path in life. We wanted to follow God in a total way, trying to live the Gospel twenty-four hours a day. Young and inexperienced and different as we were from one another, it wasn't without its problems.

One evening, because of the commitments each of us had that night, we ate a little earlier than usual. Little by little, as we were eating our meal, we began talking about the practical aspects of our living together. It was like a detailed analysis of what wasn't going right. No one named names of who was in the wrong, but in reality, it wasn't difficult to guess.

At a certain point we realized that there was a rift between us. And even though one of us said, 'It's getting late,' no one got up. We stayed there in silence until someone said he was sorry, then another and another until all of us had.

We then spoke at length, calmly and relaxed, and slowly some practical ideas emerged, which we all agreed on. We felt a great joy and realized that from that moment our little community was taking a qualitative leap forward.

By putting mutual love into action, the presence of Jesus in our midst had been restored. The words, 'Where two or more are united in my name, there am I in their midst,' resounded in our hearts.

The next morning, going to work we were sorry to leave the house. It was so good to be together now. While saying goodbye someone said, 'When you feel that there's communion, that there's unity amongst us, you feel the urge to ask the Father for anything you can think of, certain of obtaining it.'[7] It proved to be enough just to have wanted it…

---

7. 'If two of you agree on earth about anything you ask, it will be done for you by my Father in heaven.' (Mt. 18:19)

In the kitchen we had a little blackboard where we wrote down what we needed to buy. That morning before leaving one of us had written the word: *tuna*.

Later on, in the early afternoon, another one of us came home and because he particularly liked tuna, he added the word 'immediately' to the blackboard.

A couple of hours later, before leaving to do the shopping the doorbell rang: it was a woman who, through other people had heard that a community of young people were living the Gospel.

She had brought a huge box for us. She asked if we could go down and get it because it was very heavy. We opened it and what do you think we saw? Fifty tins of tuna.

P.D.R. - Rocca di Papa (Rome)

The Ideal of My Life

At many moments in my life I have found God's love to be generous and abundant, particularly after I became ill. One of the effects of chemotherapy was that I lost my hair. It is true that Jesus said, 'I was hungry and you gave me to eat, I was thirsty and you gave me to drink,' but where I am now, not long ago, I also experienced, 'I was without hair and you gave me your own.'

What happened was that three young people from the Movement had their hair cut so that I could have a wig made with hair the same colour as my own.

It was also a difficult moment from a financial point of view, not only because the treatment was expensive, but also because I was unable to work, I had lost the opportunity of teaching extra lessons that were offered to me. I was beginning to fall prey to worry. I offered everything to Mary and felt that Jesus was asking me to have faith.

After a few days, the answer came. However impossible it might seem, I received notice of my sickness benefit and it was higher than my salary. Not only that, I had been given an allowance for the extra lessons I was unable to teach!

A hymn to God rose within me. It is impossible not to believe in you, it is impossible not to make you the ideal of my life.

C. – Golania (Brazil)

For the Last Time

At Fontem, in Cameroon, Africa, land is very precious because in practice it is the only resource that people have. Indeed they live on what they produce from their land, by cultivating coffee and cocoa etc.

To build the hospital, the college and the parish church, the king of the tribe, called the Fon, gave us forty-two hectares of land. To the previous landowners he had given other plots.

According to the agreement, within a year of harvesting their various crops, the landowners were to leave. And that is what happened, apart from one. The Fon tried every way to convince him, but with no success. In that area of the land, every now and again, a new plot would be cultivated by the ex-proprietor who continued to live in the spot where a new wing of the hospital was due to be built.

A simple but dignified home had been built for him, but it wasn't enough to make him leave his land. The situation grew increasingly more difficult.

Each evening Marilen H., the person responsible for the little town that was developing, thinking that at times prayer demands persistence, would ask the Eternal Father to resolve the situation. In the meantime months and even years went by without change. After approximately ten years, one evening, as we did every other evening, we prayed with Marilen, but that evening there was a difference: 'Eternal Father, in the name of Jesus, we ask you to resolve this problem with the land; we ask you for the last time.'

The next day, to everyone's surprise, the man left the house and the land, and moved to his new house!

A.P.M. – Rocca di Papa (Rome)

A New House

I grew up in a poor area, but despite this, ever since I was a small child I dreamed of having a university degree, so that I could improve my family's living conditions.

Even though I went to work at fifteen, by studying at evening classes I managed to gain a degree in accountancy.

After getting to know the spirituality of the Movement, the vocation to leave everything and follow Jesus, in the Focolare, grew in me. And that is what I did.

A few years later I returned home to help my mother during a period of convalescence.

One evening, near my sister's house, all of a sudden gunfire broke out. While I was lying on the floor taking cover, along with my sister and nephew, I thought, 'Certainly, even if I had stayed at home and renounced my vocation, my financial help wouldn't have been enough to buy my family a place in a more settled and less dangerous place. But there is one thing I can do: pray to Jesus.'

Straight away I said to him, 'I ask you to do my part to find the way to let my nephew grow up in a better environment.'

A few months later news came that my sister had won a raffle at the supermarket: a new house right in the most sought-after area.

G. – *Belo Horizonte (Brazil)*

A Whole Ham

We were in a focolare in Poland, during the difficult times in the 1980s. It was a period of political and economic crisis and inflation was sky high. The shops were empty. Only vinegar and salt were on display on the grocery counters. Meat, sugar, bread and rice were rationed, and the queues were endless!

It was Easter. Tradition demands that as well as eggs, other foods used to celebrate Easter are also blessed, and among these cooked ham is a must. But where was it to be found?

On Easter morning, one of our relatives, quite unexpectedly, brought a small bit of ham (who knows where it had been found!) to share with us.

We remembered some of our young friends who we were certain would have very little to put on their table for Easter, and we decided to give the ham to them.

A little later the doorbell rang. Someone who knew us wanted to share a some ham. Again no one knew how or where or how long it took to queue up to get it.

We were happy, but then thought of a family who were very faithful to the traditions. After a moment's thought we decided to give this ham to them.

A very short time elapsed, and there was another knock on the door. This time we were offered a whole ham!

The Gospel is true, 'Give, and it will be given!'

D.F. - Italy

The Exact Amount and More...

At the end of a meeting, a woman approached me and in obvious embarrassment, and confided that financially she was going through a very difficult moment. She needed to find three million lire straight away because she had to repay an old debt to the bank. She had been paying interest on it for a long time without ever being able to repay any of the capital. The bank had decided to withdraw her credit, and she had to close the account immediately. Her husband was working for a company that had not paid him in months. Her son, who served as a volunteer for a charitable organization, had a poorly paid job on which the family survived.

This woman's problem became my own. We were in the little garden belonging to some nuns and next to it was the small chapel. I said to her, 'Let's go and talk to Jesus.' The woman, however, expected a different solution. But I was sure of what I had suggested to her. Kneeling in front of the tabernacle, I explained the situation to Jesus out loud. While I was speaking she wept. Leaving the chapel I saw she was calm and showed great faith in God.

A few days later she telephoned and announced that, out of the blue, she had received news in the post that her husband's pay arrears, which had mounted up over several months, were about to be paid. The money had only to be collected: it covered the full amount needed cancel the debt, with a little more just to keep them going.

P. D. - Italy

The Geography Exam

I was studying for my teaching diploma and I had to take one last Geography exam, which consisted of a practical lesson, on a subject of my own choice, given in front of a panel to children. I was well prepared on the agriculture of a region in Spain and I had lots of teaching aids, so that the children would be able to see and understand what I was talking about better.

I was waiting for my turn. At a certain moment another student teacher asked me which subject I had prepared. I explained and showed her what I had with me. She told me that she too had chosen the same lesson but didn't have anything to show to the children and, realizing how important it was, asked me for one or two objects. Even though I had tried to love Jesus in her, she was the person with whom I had the least relationship; on many occasions she had been very distant with me. She came from a higher class and didn't do anyone any favours and so I didn't particularly like her. She would have been the last person I would have given anything to. Besides this I was worried that if I had less material, my own presentation wouldn't be as good. It was a difficult moment for me. But I remembered throughout that it was Jesus, and felt that I had to love her as myself.

I gave her half of what I had.

I remember the happiness I felt within. It was pure joy: I had been able to love Jesus despite everything!

The moment of the exam came. I gave my presentation with what I had left. When the marks were announced I realized that I had the highest. So perhaps Jesus was pleased.

A.S. - Spain

Unconditional Faith

A friend of mine was put in prison for something he hadn't done. For a long time many of us prayed for him and did everything we could to obtain his freedom, but the situation remained difficult.

One night I couldn't sleep. The words, 'Ask with faith and you will receive,' kept coming back to me.

I think that I had never yet prayed with the faith Jesus intended: unconditional faith. I knelt down and turning to him, spontaneously I said, 'I am praying to you for my friend; I am certain that he will be set free tomorrow.'

A few hours elapsed and I received a telephone call. My friend had been set free. A solution had been found for him.

I put down the receiver with inexpressible emotion.

S.L. - Italy

All Were My Size

I am a girl from Valencia. Having come from another country I realized that my friends at school didn't like the way I dressed. Because there are lots of children in my family, there was nothing my parents could do about it, so I decided not to worry but to leave it all to our Father who is in heaven. After two weeks the clothing came: a pair of shoes, a blouse, some trousers and a jacket, all were new and in my size!

A. - Valencia (Spain)

More Than Was Needed

I come from Tanzania and I'm almost blind. The person who helps me to study also gave me 1,200 shillings to buy a malaria injection, so that I could finish the treatment I had started.

I was going towards the pharmacy.

A poor woman stopped me and told me of her needs. What I had on me was what I needed but – because I saw Jesus in her – I felt I should help her. And so I gave her two hundred shillings. When I reached the pharmacy, I saw an old woman who was in pain: she didn't have enough money to buy the medicine, which she more than needed.

I helped her as well with two hundred shillings.

Giving and giving, I found myself in the same situation as the two women I had helped. I now needed four hundred shillings. But I was certain God was watching and looking after everything.

I went in the pharmacy and met a friend. After greeting me he asked why I was there. I explained simply, 'Recently, having been very ill, I have been having injections and I now need the last one which I have come to buy.'

Without knowing anything about my situation, my friend handed me five hundred shillings. My heart was filled with joy: now I had more than enough for what I needed. What happened was further proof that I should never be frightened of sharing what I have with others. The Lord, in his infinite love, will take care of us.

A boy from Tanzania

The Gift of a Doll

I am a young girl from Porto Alegre in Brazil.

I had a doll, which I liked very much, but when I got to know a poor girl who didn't have one, I gave mine to her. I reminded myself that Jesus was in that little girl and that I could give the doll to Jesus. So that's what I did.

The next day, one of my neighbours gave me a big parcel, which contained lots of wonderful toys and even some dolls. I was really happy and I gave more gifts to some poor children.

G.G. - Porto Alegre (Brazil)

Until We Meet Again in Heaven

Maria, someone I knew, still grieved because of her father's death, even though several years had gone by.

One day, as I passed a bookshop, I noticed a well-written book, which was beautifully illustrated with the title: *Until We Meet Again in Heaven*. I thought that it was appropriate for her and I bought it. But then for various reasons the book stayed at home for a time, as I either didn't know what to write in it or I kept forgetting to deliver it. In the end I decided to send it by post despite the cost.

One day I received a telephone call. Maria was amazed by the gift, which arrived precisely on the anniversary of her father's departure for heaven. That morning she had dared to ask him for a sign. She seemed to have found it when she opened the packet and read: *Until We Meet Again in Heaven!*

M.V. - Belgium

Why Doubt?

A few days ago a mechanic warned me that the old car used by our focolare had reached the end of its days and was no longer safe to run. It wasn't worth repairing it.

Because we needed it to go to work, however, each day, during evening prayers, we all asked Jesus for a car.

As it didn't come straight away, at a certain point we began to think about buying a second-hand car, but while we were figuring out the costs to see if this were feasible, a beautiful new car arrived, given by one of our relatives.

From now on we don't want to doubt Jesus.

C.d.M. - Valencia (Spain)

You Are Asking Too Much of Me, Jesus

Angelo, a friend who found himself unemployed, told me of an enormous suffering for him: the death of his newly born daughter. When I left him I had a great desire to do something for him. The next day my first thought was to find a job for Angelo.

Amongst the very few possibilities in a country with high unemployment, Carlo, another friend, came to mind, as he was a manager in a very large company.

But the day I wanted to do this I was so busy that I realized I wouldn't be able to contact him. During the mass I was moaning a little to Jesus, 'You are asking too much of me!'

While I was walking along the road, to meet up with a person who is confronting a very sad situation – one of the jobs I had to do that day – I entrusted Angelo's work to God.

With great peace I listened to that person until finally he was comforted and cheered.

When I returned home there was a message. It was from Angelo: he had found a job. He was delighted and I was too. But the second thing he said truly moved me. The post was in Carlo's firm. Angelo had come into contact with him by another means.

X.Z. - Italy

The Sound Mixer Breaks Down

During a sports festival, with a thousand children from the Movement present, all of a sudden the sound mixer broke down.

While I was talking on the telephone to a technician, trying to work out how to fix it, Pablo, a seven year-old boy, came up to me. Seeing by my face that I was worried, he asked me, 'Do you have a problem with the sound?'

In my near desperation, which his question only made worse, I said to him, 'Look, Pablo. As Jesus listens more to children than to adults, ask him to fix this mixer.' And I continued my conversation with the technician.

Not even thirty seconds later, the sound came back on, having followed an instruction given by the technician, and it made a tremendous noise in the field where we were.

Straight away I looked at Pablo, who was next to me and he, with surprise and joy, said to me, 'I've only just asked Jesus!'

D.R. – Buenos Aires

At the Time of Solidarnosc

It was in the 1980s in Poland to which the Movement had spread.

It was in the years of *Solidarnosc*, with a struggle going on against the system; a time of strong government repression. There were arrests, searches, and police roadblocks at almost every corner.

In the focolare there were writings, tape recordings and videocassettes: what was to be done? At any moment the police could have come to our door too. As much as we could we tried to get everything away to safety.

Andrzej, a focolarino, loaded everything into the boot of the car and left for a safe place. But, after a few yards he came to a police roadblock: scores of cars were being closely searched one after another!

What was he to do? He couldn't turn back. All that remained was for him to pray and wait with his heart in his mouth!

When it was his turn, Andrzej, from the depth of his soul appealed to Mary, 'Look out for us, I cannot do anything. The Movement is yours!'[8]

The policeman looked at the focolarino, greeted him and waved him on. It was the only car not to be checked.

S.A. - Poland

I Am An Atheist, But You Must Be Mad

One day Carlo, a friend, came to see me and confided in me about a great suffering. His parents were on the point of divorce because of his father's unfaithfulness during a work trip abroad.

Apart from the suffering from seeing his parents' love for one another grow less, he found the thought that someone else would choose which parent he had to live with, unbearable, separating him from his only brother, of whom he was very fond.

I was caught up with the situation and felt a great sadness which wouldn't go away.

What is more, Carlo was an atheist and I didn't want to make the situation worse by talking to him of God. I would risk not being understood.

I was with Carlo when some words from the commentary from that month's Word of Life came to mind: 'The Word of God lived can burst, like a river in full flood, over what seems insurmountable.' This was the light that cleared away the darkness and eventually

---

8. The Focolare Movement is also called the Work of Mary.

helped me recognize the face of Jesus crucified and forsaken in Carlo, and gave me the strength to say to him, 'As a Christian I would offer my suffering to God, putting the problem into his hands, so that his will may be fully done, in the certainty that whatever happens in the future would be for my own good.'

He replied, 'I am an atheist, but you must be truly mad!'

I didn't lose heart and insisted: 'Be brave, it's worth trying. Say to Jesus quite simply, "I am placing this suffering in your hands." And then be calm and wait for what will happen.'

Before he left for home, I told him he could telephone me at any time if he needed help. When he left the storm in his heart certainly hadn't abated.

The next day, to my great joy, I received a telephone call to say that Carlo had felt compelled, in desperation, to give his suffering to God.

I felt he was comforted. After another two days I received another call in which he told me there was no longer to be a divorce or any separation from his brother.

His mother had found the strength to forgive his father and the two of them had been reconciled.

S.D. - Trent

A Family Rebuilt

Armelle's mother had left the Church and was living a disorderly life, abusing alcohol and other things, because her husband had left her to live with another woman.

Each Sunday, when his mother took Armelle and his sister, who was still a child, to his father's, he remembered to put on his best clothes to go to mass and once there he and his sister entrusted his father and his mother to Jesus.

Armelle's mother, profoundly moved by her children's attitude, returned to the sacraments and gave up the bad company she had been keeping.

After a few months his father began going home to see all three of them more often, and struck by the atmosphere and the change in his wife, he left the other woman and returned to his own family.

And very soon they went back to Church together.

G.L. - Burkina Faso

At the Iron Works

I had been in the Ivory Coast for several years, when it became necessary for me to go for a month's trip to Togo, to visit the Movement's community, spread throughout that country.

In the weeks before I was due to leave our little town, however, work at the iron works was in short supply.

How could I go, leaving behind two workers, family men, without work or any wages for a month or two, or who knows for how long?

There were three days to go and still there wasn't any work. That evening, at mass, in agreement with another focolarino we asked Jesus.

In the morning, with some trepidation, I went to the iron works. It was the beginning of the year and passing by the printing press I realized I hadn't greeted the workers, all friends of mine, who worked in that little business. And so, remembering that it was my duty as a focolarino to put love of God and of my neighbour at the basis of every other thing, I decided, even though it was late, to go and see them.

Amongst others I greeted an elderly missionary who had come to make some photocopies. I knew him only by sight, but I stopped to talk to him, exchange greetings and ask about what he was doing.

He had been in Africa for more than forty years and was due to return to France shortly, but before leaving he wanted to build a church in the last village where he was now parish priest. Within half an hour we had agreed on some work which was needed: doors, windows, window bars... all made of iron! Yes, because there are many termites in that area and they eat through wood in no time. As he left, he gave me an advance with which to buy the materials.

I had just enough time to prepare the measurements and the plans to start the job off and to buy the materials.

The work lasted for six months and was well paid, more than we could have dared to ask for.

Great was the workers' joy and my gratitude to Jesus for having listened to our prayers.

R.C. - Ivory Coast

The Courage to Uphold Your Principles

Patricia, a twenty-two year-old law student, worked in a Ministry in Paraguay: 'I met the spirituality of unity when I was small,' she recounts, 'and throughout these years it has become my way of life.'

For some time she held the post of Head of Department. 'From the beginning,' she confided, 'I aimed always to do well in work and foster relationships with my colleagues so that each one would feel valued. I tried to be loving, discovering the face of Jesus in each person, in my colleagues and in those who came to the office.'

The bond with her colleagues grew. 'My wish to do things differently from how they are done in other public offices became the norm for them too. People were surprised by the way they were treated. They felt listened to and had the certainty that their problems would be dealt with when the time was right.'

But for Patricia it meant going against the stream to uphold her principles whatever the consequences. She tells the story. 'An important person at my place of work, who enjoyed certain privileges, behaved dishonestly. And to justify it he put forward this argument: "If you have decided to become a lawyer and don't do anything illegal you are wasting time and you will end up quite simply, dead of hunger." I felt, however, that this wasn't true. There are many people who live, as I want to live. I had to tell him so, with charity certainly, but I had to do it. I felt within me the certainty that it was "love" to tell someone what isn't right.'

For having shown her convictions, Patricia lost her job.

'I suffered terribly, but at the same time I was relaxed, because I knew I had acted in the right way.'

She didn't despair since she was very conscious of having a Father for whom everything is possible and who loved her without measure. He who looks after the birds of the air would look after her.

It seemed impossible in the economic and work climate in Paraguay and yet that same evening two offers of work arrived, and she arranged an interview for the next day.

In addition, the new job had more direct links with her studies and was therefore more interesting and useful for her personal development.

With infinite gratitude in her heart, she said, 'It's a new challenge opening up for me and offering me thousands of opportunities to live and to serve.'

P.C. - Paraguay

From a Heart of Stone to One of Flesh

My husband's mother was very fond of her son, to the point of being jealous, and this attitude has always created difficulties between us.

A year ago she was diagnosed as having a tumour. This necessitated home care that her only daughter was unable to give.

About that time, after being invited by a friend, I took part in a Mariapolis[9] and the meeting with God who is love[10] changed my life.

The first consequence of this conversion was the decision to overcome my every fear and invite my mother-in-law into my home. The light in my heart,

---

9. Summer meeting of the Focolare Movement
10. For the members of the Movement the first point in understanding the spirituality that animates it, is the discovery that God loves us immensely.

which had been lit during the meeting, made me see her with new eyes. Now I knew it was Jesus in her whom I was helping and looking after. Little by little my heart of stone became a heart of flesh.

She was not indifferent to my love, and matched my acts of love with ones of her own. The grace of God worked the miracle of reciprocity!

Months of sacrifice, which didn't weigh me down, went by, and when my mother-in-law went serenely to heaven, we were all very peaceful.

About that time I realized I was expecting a baby, something I had wanted for nine years. This child is for us a tangible sign of God's love, in exchange for the little bit of love given the child's grandmother.

M. - Argentina

The Rocking Chair

The week before Mother's Day I paid some bills and checked our bank account.

I explained to my husband, Dean, that I had paid the car insurance with the credit card and that there was only enough money to pay the rent the next Tuesday. He wasn't to spend a single penny until that day.

On Sunday, Mother's Day, I stayed in bed for a bit, and the children brought me a cup of tea, some biscuits and a card, which they had made for me.

Dean really wanted to give me a rocking chair that day, but he was happy that we had shared our financial difficulties.

Later on we went to see the children's grandmother who was clearing out a room for another granddaughter who was going to live with her. Turning to me she said, 'Would you like to take the rocking chair?'

I, who on many occasions had asked my husband for one before a new baby was born, was delighted. And Dean, opening up his heart to tell me of his wish, told me, happily, of having seen the hand of providence.

I.S. - Melbourne (Australia)

Now You're Coming With Me...

I live in Rio de Janeiro, one of the most beautiful cities in the world. In the Movement we try to live out a Word of the Gospel for a period of time. To do this there is a commentary on a sheet of paper, which is translated into ninety-one languages and sent out each month to those who know the Movement throughout the world.

One night I left work a little late, but I didn't want to go home until I had delivered the last copy of the Word of Life commentary to a family I visit each month. So I telephoned my mother to tell her my intentions. To be quick, I thought I would take a taxi.

In the rear-view mirror I could see the taxi driver's face. He said to me, 'You got into the wrong car. This taxi's stolen. Now you're coming with me.'

I shuddered: Is he a rapist? Where is he going to take me?

The taxi made its way out of the city. We arrived in front of a motel, a brothel, and he made me get out, pushing me into a room. While he was outside in the hall, I sat on the bed. What was going to happen to me? It might be my last moment of life. It was then that I thought of the Word of Life, which I was carrying, and I began to read it slowly.

The man came in and closed the door. He sat next to me and put his arm on my shoulder. 'What are you doing?' he asked.

I told him that it was a commentary on the Gospel, words of Jesus, which I try to live.

'Read it out loud to me!' he said aggressively.

I thought I should live that moment with solemnity, reading word by word with love. I hadn't reached the end of the page when he snatched the sheet from my hands and said, 'Go, go away, you're too good!'

The Word had saved me.

M.A.C.- Rio de Janeiro

A Letter Containing Fifteen Thousand Francs

I arrived in Montet, Switzerland, in 1981, to give a hand in rebuilding a new little town, called Mariapolis 'Foco', which the next year would house the men and women focolarini in the second year of their training.

The major works having been completed, essential equipment needed to be provided, and there wasn't any money. Nevertheless, one day, moved by love for the focolarine, I went to a firm to buy sixty chairs for the dining rooms in the focolares, where there were only tables. I would have to pay the invoice for seven thousand francs within 30 days.

I was on the way back to Montet, and after a worried moment, I entrusted the situation to the Eternal Father, certain that he would do something.

A few days later an anonymous letter arrived. Inside there was a small envelope. I opened it. It contained fifteen thousand francs, without a word, and not even a signature.

Eighteen years later, we still don't know which person the Eternal Father used to send us that money.

P.F. - Montet (Switzerland)

So It Works!

My twenty-year-old son wanted a mobile phone, because, as he wanted to give lessons, he thought he could be contacted more easily. He spoke of a phone, which was on offer, and kept mentioning it so that I would buy it for him. As I couldn't afford it, it came to mind to suggest he asked providence for it.

He agreed, but wasn't too convinced, whereas I was certain that if it was the will of God it would come.

After a while news came that a company where my friend worked was closing down, and he let us know that he was giving us two mobile phones. When my son heard this he exclaimed, 'So it works! This way, my brother will get a mobile phone as well!'

J.G. - Hungary

A Flower Vase

I had only just left my family to follow Jesus as a focolarina. When I lived at home, one of the things I liked doing best was to go to the focolare with flowers, perhaps paying for them with money saved by skipping a snack. Now that I was in the focolare I could no longer do this.

But during that period many flowers began arriving... every day. One day there were so many we didn't have enough vases for them. I said to Jesus, 'Thank you! You are a real gentlemen, but that's enough flowers. We don't have any more vases.' The doorbell rang. A man had brought as a gift for the focolare a beautiful... vase for flowers!

N.C. - Loppiano (Florence)

Love Conquers Everything

I am a gynaecologist and the mother of six children. The other evening, before going to a doctor's meeting, while I was driving home one of my youngest, the little boy, exclaimed, 'Mummy, I love you so much. What would happen to us if you weren't here?'

I reassured him straight away.

Later, while I was parking the car at the entrance to the Polyclinic, three armed youths beckoned me to get out. At the time it seemed like a joke. But then, one boy, pushing his revolver into my neck, made it clear that it was serious. 'If you don't get out, I'll kill you!'

I climbed out of the car, and as one of them took the steering wheel, I realized that they were going to take me away. My son's words thumped in my heart. I felt I had reached the moment to take a decisive step, to make a new choice of God.[11] I presumed that they might be my last moments and I had to live them well, with love alone. I did this and I felt a great sense of peace in my soul.

I took an interest in them as a mother would. They wanted money and when they heard that I had six children and was a doctor, they stopped talking so much. There was a long silence while the car raced out of the city. Then, 'Lady, don't worry, nothing is going to happen to you. Your car will be found soon!'

At one point, because of a difference of opinion, they started arguing, using harsh words and threatening one another with a revolver. I kept my head lowered, trying not to look at them, praying for them. They were little older than my older children....

Finally they stopped, and left me on foot in the middle of the countryside. I walked for twenty minutes looking for a path, which would lead me to a tarmac road and a telephone. I called my husband to come and pick me up. The adventure had come to an end!

The next day the car was returned: inside were my bags with my documentation, money, cheque book and tape recorder... and not a scratch on the bodywork.

T.N. - Brazil

---

11. This means to put God in the first place in one's life and, as an expression of that, to love one's neighbour.

An Exceptional Gift

It was in the nineteen eighties. At that time the formation meetings for members of the Movement, which were held at the Mariapolis Centre in Rocca di Papa, had increased to the point of having to use a building belonging to another organization, a few kilometres away, to accommodate additional meetings. We were compelled to divide up into two groups for the same meeting, as the numbers were more than double the capacity of the meeting hall. This saddened us especially because it wasn't in keeping with our desire for unity, which is a fundamental characteristic of our Movement.

Our spontaneous reaction was to start searching for a meeting hall for 2,000 people in the area surrounding the zone of Castelli.

But, first of all, we prayed. Chiara began to entrust it to God in unity with us, in the knowledge that, as the Gospel says, in that way our prayer would be better heard.

We are children of the Father. And we had no doubt he would look after us, but we could never have envisaged, at that time, how much.

We then began knocking on lots of doors. We were listened to, suggestions were made, but that was all.

We even found something on one site, which made us cherish for a while the idea of building a complete new construction, corresponding to our needs. But this dream came to nothing for reasons of bureaucracy.

What happened to Mary and Joseph when they were looking for a place for their Son who was soon to be born, kept coming to mind. It was at this stage, on 5 December 1982, when the annual meeting for the women focolarine began, that we received a telephone call from the Vatican's Secretary of State.

We were called to the Vatican and told that the Holy Father was offering us the hall where he held his audiences at Castel Gandolfo, a hall, which could hold at least three thousand people!

In those years Chiara had had been very keen on the idea of erecting a type of 'cathedral to Jesus in the midst for those gathered together in his name' and now it seemed that the Eternal Father was giving us a hand to make it a reality.

The joy for Chiara and for us was immense, also because God's providence, timely and tangible, came to us by means of the Holy Father.

In almost three years, thanks to the contribution of a thousand lire a month (there are lots of us) we were able to remodel it completely, transforming a huge chamber a hundred and ten metres long and twelve metres high into a three storey building with two halls containing twelve hundred and eighteen hundred seats respectively, which by opening partition walls can become a single hall. Other than this we built a dining room able to provide twelve hundred meals, as well as a small number of rooms to be used as bedrooms. It was all far more than our highest expectations!

That year Chiara ended by sending us the following message:

'The huge hall, which the Pope has offered to us, is a tangible gift that God is sending to us. It is his love on the occasion of the Movement's fortieth anniversary. We are grateful to him!

D.Z. - Rocca di Papa (Rome)

It Could Have Been An Iron

I was in the focolare in Bilbao when it first opened and it needed lots of things, but we were happy. Jesus in the midst, through our mutual love, was such that we weren't even aware of what we needed. Almost every day we were amazed by the useful things that we saw come from the small community around us.

One day, I realized that in one of our other focolare centre's, the one where Luminosa lived, they needed an electric mixer. As it was my birthday the following month my family had asked me what I would like them to give me, and I had asked for a mixer.

When it came, very happily, I took it to Luminosa, who didn't want to accept it because we needed one too. But then, out of love for us, she accepted it.

Some time later, a lady came to our focolare. She had been on holiday at her mother's house in the country in the south of Spain. She brought us homemade olive oil and another parcel.

What a surprise we had when we opened it, to find an electric mixer identical to the one we had given to Luminosa.

We felt like rejoicing! We said, 'You could have brought us an iron, or drinking glasses, or a tablecloth… but no! A mixer! "Give and it will be given."'

A.S. - Spain

A Well Packed Box

Where we live it is very hot and you have to drink a lot. For this reason we really wanted a blender to make fruit drinks. We didn't have money to buy one, but we asked it of the Eternal Father.

One day some of our Muslim friends came to visit us and brought us a gift: a well packed box. We opened it: a blender!

M.C. - Tanzania

The 'Sweetener'

My colleague and I have a little company that imports medical equipment. It is very expensive and so it's not easy to make sales. Unfortunately, in public hospitals it is the practice to give the people responsible for making the purchase a 'sweetener'. My colleague and I don't go along with this practice, and so we have lost out on potential sales.

At a very difficult time, when there had been few sales, one of our salesmen came to my office to tell me that to pull off a sale – on the point of completion – a person from the office who was buying was asking for a 'sweetener' from us. I realized that for our salesman it was very important to go ahead with the deal, because he received a percentage as part of his salary. Calmly, I spoke clearly to him, explaining my principles, that this would be a corrupt act, and that even though we might profit from it, it was not part of our company's policy.

He left the office thoughtfully, but returned later decisive: he would not make the sale under those conditions.

That same afternoon the telephone rang. It was a doctor with whom we had been trying to finalize a very big sale for some time but who kept putting it off. Out of the blue he confirmed that he was buying our product: the cost was exactly ten times more than the sale which hadn't gone ahead.

When I put down the telephone, surprised and happy, I remembered with what had happened a few hours earlier, the words of Jesus, 'Seek first the kingdom of God and its justice and the rest will be given to you as well.'

I was happy to share the great joy I was experiencing straight away with our salesman, so that he too could touch God's providence.

J.B. - Buenos Aires

The Situation Was Turned Round

On his fifth birthday, Frederick, the youngest of our six children, was struck down with a very serious illness. There was only one diagnosis: septic meningitis. After a few days the doctors made us realize that the situation was now extremely serious. They were expecting him to collapse and perhaps go into kidney failure.

We came together to pray and to ask, if it was God's will, for him to recover. We also asked for the community to pray. All of us felt that we were participating in this suffering and we began a chain of prayer: with faith, asking united with one another, all things can be had. Within a few hours and to the great surprise of the doctor on duty, the situation changed completely. The next day our son was out of danger and the head of the ward told us to thank 'someone' because a miracle had occurred.

A.M. - Rome

Fifty-Four Litres of Oil

I had not long been in the focolare in Gitega, Burundi. In the town, which is still small and has few shops, it's not always easy to find all that one needs to live.

One morning a woman, who was poor and sick, knocked at our door.

When I opened the door to her, with a big smile she asked for a little oil. Going into the kitchen I realized that what was there was insufficient to make lunch for the other focolarine and there wasn't any in the shops. I wanted to keep the little I had, but Jesus' voice within told me to give it away. I felt that the loving thing to do was to seek the kingdom of God. I went into the room to consult with Agnes, another focolarina, who hadn't yet left for work. Together we decided to say yes, and that's what we did.

I started to work and at eleven o'clock I went into the kitchen to prepare lunch. Remembering that we didn't have any oil, I said to myself: 'OK I can cook without oil, what matters is that we have loved.'

There wasn't even time for me to pick up a pan when someone came to the door. I went to open it and there was a nun we hadn't seen for some time because she lives in a far-away district. She said to me, 'Come with me to the car.' There she gave me three large cans of oil, which in total contained fifty-four litres!

Gitega (Burundi)

Writing From Chicago

One day I went to the shoe shop. My youngest son needed a pair of size 3 wide-fit. As this type of shoe is not very common, I searched the shop until... there they were, the exact size I needed! Not only that, they were a style and colour that were really nice! With my son in my arms and the shoes in my hand I went to the cash desk to buy them. It was only at that moment that I remembered that the month's finances hadn't been too good and I wouldn't have enough money. I made my apologies, put the shoes down and left.

With tears in my eyes, I then set off to meet a friend. I knew that she would be glad of a chat. On the way there I said, 'Jesus, I am not asking anything for myself, but for my son!' In my heart I felt certain that he would take care of everything!

When I arrived at my friend's I hadn't even had time to greet her when she said, 'You won't believe what happened today. I found this pair of shoes that perhaps your son may be able to use! I opened the parcel: not only were they size 3 wide-fit, but they were the exact style and colour of those I had left behind in the shop!

P.R. - Chicago

Excellent Marks

Once, at the same time as there was a congress for young people of the Movement in Rome, which I really wanted to go to, I had to take my final exams to go to university. They fell the day after my return. The teacher, who was responsible for my course, knowing what I wanted to do, counselled me against it, telling me I was gambling with my future.

But it was *my* congress and I couldn't miss it.

And so I abandoned myself to God, convinced that if I did my part, he would do his and all would go well.

In the preceding days I studied very hard.

On my return I studied again, calmly and with great peace. I did the same the next morning, before the exam.

Surprise! The questions in the exam were on *exactly* the few things that I had revised the night before I went to the congress, and my marks were excellent.

A.M.V.N. – Spain

Like the Early Days

One Saturday someone came to pay us a short visit. When she was leaving, knowing that she had many children and that financially things weren't going too well, we from the women's focolare gave her all the fruit we had in the house: all we had for the week.

After a while another family visited us and, as they had been to the market, they offered us fresh apples and pears. We were happy because we saw it as the 'give and it will be given to you' from the Gospel.

In the afternoon, as an act of love, we had promised to go to a party organized by the local Italian community. We had decided on the way to visit another needy family and take them all the apples and pears we had received. Once the party was over, before we left, the family who had invited us gave us a large box full of pears and apples from their orchard, all of excellent quality, along with a huge watermelon.

We were delighted that these experiences should happen not only in the early days of the Movement, but today too. The words, 'Give and it will be given in full measure…' are for all times.

A.S.S.L. – New Zealand

After Ten Minutes on the Telephone

I was asked to collect a V.I.P. from his hotel and take him to the airport. Happy to be of service, I set off. But, alas, at a narrow stretch of the road, another car travelling at speed met me head on. I was able to get out of the way just in time, but I had scratched the back of the car against the wall next to the road. What was I to do? I had to go on to keep my appointment. I needed therefore to forget for the moment what had happened, to concentrate my mind and my heart on my passenger. We had such a good talk that as he left we greeted each other very warmly.

On my return home I confessed my small accident to a friend and together we offered everything to God. As a student, I didn't have enough to have the car repaired.

Only ten minutes later I received a telephone call. It was an aunt, who had never done anything like this before, who wanted to give me a sum of money. It was what I needed for the repair.

C.T., Seminarian – Italy

A New Water Mattress

I work in a government department, which is responsible for helping the disabled. One day I was asked to contact a family, which was in a difficult situation, to see if I could do anything.

I telephoned the man and he explained that his wife had a malignant tumour and was in urgent need of a water mattress.

I set about looking for one, but it proved very difficult. This type of donation is rare and is expensive.

Every time a situation like this occurs I think that it is Jesus in that particular person, who has a need, and I try to help him. But this time in spite of having done all I could, I hadn't found anything. In the meantime the family telephoned me several times, very upset. For me too it was a hard suffering.

One morning, while I was on the bus going to work, I remembered the experience, which Chiara has told many times: 'The size 42 shoes'.

Straight away, even though I was with lots of people, I prayed to Jesus that he would find a water mattress for me. I seemed to feel a certainty that he would respond and I left everything in his hands.

In the afternoon, after a directors' meeting in the bureau where I work, as I was leaving, I was called over. The directors wanted to give me a parcel.

It contained a new water mattress! Not only that, but also a very good cream for the lady who was ill!

Together with a colleague I rushed to the family and you can imagine with what joy and gratitude they were received.

L.F.V. – Costa Rica

A Suspended Contract

It was a time when there was little work at the printing works in the little town of El Diamante[12] in Mexico, and every day we asked the Eternal Father for clients.

A young person visiting the little town was struck by what she saw and arranged an appointment with someone who worked for a very big film company, Twentieth Century Fox. He was director of marketing for the whole of Latin America. We were overjoyed.

When we met the director, we showed him our range of products and immediately he ordered a print run of thousands of key rings for the premiere of a film. We discussed dates, prices, etc. and he promised that there would be work in the future.

We could see that it would cover salaries for the next two months, but before finalizing the contract I asked him what the film was about. After only a few words I

---

12. El Diamante, like Loppiano in Italy, is one of the Focolare little towns.

realized that it was not in line with our principles, and I suspended the contract.

Incredulous, the director insisted; he couldn't imagine that someone would refuse business of this kind. But I remembered the words: 'Seek first the Kingdom of God and his justice, and these other things will be given you as well.' (Mt. 6:33).

On our return to the little town, we explained what had happened to the others, who were happy that we had been faithful to our principles, even though it would mean a real effort just to survive.

We didn't have to wait long for God's answer. The next day the telephone rang and we were offered a year's work printing children's T-shirts with our own designs.

T.C. – Mexico

Just Right

A pair of shoes had arrived in the focolare. They were beautiful, new and with high heels... but tiny: size 33. 'Who knows who could make use of these!' I asked myself. Soon after, someone came to the door. It was Wilma, a young woman who was very poor, who came to see us from time to time with her little girl.

Wilma is tiny, very small. Automatically I looked at her feet and I offered her the shoes.

To her great joy they fitted perfectly!

Sometimes a poor person comes along and God sends just the right providence. Other times providence comes followed by the poor person... just right.

N.C. – Loppiano (Florence)

Give to Caesar What Belongs to Caesar

In Brazil, each month, employers must deposit a percentage of their employees' salary in the bank, as insurance for the period of their employment. The employer of one company, which I dealt with, had not been paying in as much as he should have. He then had to pay what he owed as well as a huge fine to the State. He put a proposition to me that, instead of paying the fine he could pay the same sum directly to the employees, along with what he owed them.

To tell you the truth, at the time I was tempted to accept his proposition, because the fine was far higher than the missing contributions and it would have been to the employees' advantage, but even more important to me were Jesus' words, 'Give to Caesar what belongs to Caesar …'

As a Christian I had to be a living witness to his words. In response, I felt that the employer respected me for the position I had taken.

MDR. F.C. – Brazil

A Special Bicycle

One of our children, who is seven, has always been attentive to the needs of others, especially to those of other children in the world.

One day when he received twenty francs from his older brother he decided to set it aside for a mountain bike.

A few months later, at table, we were talking about the situation of some families and their children who were in great difficulty. Without saying a word, my son went to find his moneybox, gave all that it contained, and was very happy.

At times we had spoken to him about the words in the Gospel, 'Give and it will be given,' of how God gives to us when we give generously. We had emphasized that the words 'will be given' may mean the gift of joy that we feel in our heart. We did this so that he would not expect anything else.

But clearly, this was not God's thought. A couple of days later, out of the blue, a friend telephoned to ask if we needed a mountain bike, because he had received two. One was fine, but the other was too big for their eldest son.

You can imagine what joy there was in our house. It was the best bicycle we'd ever seen!

X.X. – France

As an Inspector

I am a lawyer and I work for the Ministry of Employment. One day, when I went to inspect a firm accused of not paying its employees the legal wage, I presented the summons to the owner who, taking a defensive position, argued that it was an accusation without legal foundation. But everything led me to believe that I was faced with an irregular situation.

After a fortnight of constant searching, by chance I found a document, which showed up the firm's irregularities. I was shocked. At that moment the Gospel, which asks us to love everyone, as does the heavenly Father who sends the rain on the good and on the bad, seemed like a utopia. I could not believe that someone could have acted in this way. In front of Jesus in the Eucharist, however, I asked for the strength to be faithful to his words and to be an instrument of his love.

The next day, when I showed the proprietor the evidence I had discovered, he remained stony-faced. He then said that he had taken this action because he didn't like what the State was doing to companies, forcing them to pay very high taxes, and then not using them for the common good. I replied that our errors could not be justification for the inconsistencies of others. An in-depth conversation followed, where I discovered that fundamentally, the director had the same desire for justice and equality as I had, but he had been influenced by the environment in which he lived.

Finally he said to me, 'You could have humiliated me and crushed me, but you didn't. For this reason I feel I have the confidence to start again. I hope that you will be able to come back at a later date and see that I am not what I was before.'

I replied that I had to carry out my duty and impose a fine.

I had another commitment, however, and I didn't have time to draw up the official document for him to sign. He took a blank piece of paper and signed it as it was. It was real proof that he wanted to change.

MDR. F.C. - Brazil

Blessed Illness

I am suffering from a serious illness. My kidneys have not been working properly for more than ten years and I am forced to undergo dialysis three times a week. As time goes by other organs begin to fail too.

A few days ago when I was in extreme pain, I complained to Jesus that it was a cursed illness. But soon afterwards I felt him reproach me.

'No, Luigi, it isn't cursed, quite the opposite, this illness is blessed, because thanks to this, you and I are much closer.'

How true were those words! Thinking about it, I would not change this illness for anything in the world. I thanked him.

But then I had the thought, 'I would like to go out and "evangelize" as I did when I was young!'

The very next day, a priest, whom I had met at work, said, 'The word of God is really spreading in my diocese!'

He was referring to a video prepared for Jubilee 2000, which had been distributed throughout ninety parishes in the diocese, and that contained, among the various testimonies, my witness about my illness.

What joy I felt! With my heart full of happiness and my eyes full of tears, I said to Jesus, 'How sensitive you are, how thoughtful is your love! Not even twenty-four hours have gone by and already you have answered me!'

L. D. - Buenos Aries

The Poorest Priest

A priest who was poor, told us that he wanted to go to Italy to attend a meeting for priests who belong to our Movement, but he didn't have the money to go. He trusted in providence, thinking, 'If it is God's will, he will ensure that the money comes.'

One day, when opening the post and thinking it contained the usual junk mail, he saw a cheque drop out of the envelope. It was from the diocese advising him of the death of an elderly priest, who wanted to leave some money 'to the poorest priest in the diocese', and the bishop had thought of him. It contained the exact amount that he needed to go to the meeting for priests in Rome.

M. C. - Hong Kong

Private or State School

Each month we work out our family budget, trying to involve our four children, who range in age from three to thirteen.

Together with them we try to do our best to not spend more than is necessary, so that, at one point, we thought we had reduced our necessities to the minimum. Because of the difficult financial situation the country is in, however, we have seen our income decrease to the point, lately, that we have not been able to cover even the minimum. What were we to do?

Above all we have looked for his kingdom, trying to increase our mutual love, so that Jesus among us could show us with his light what to do![13] We looked at everything again, certain that we would find the way to trim some of the expenditure, which we considered necessary. In our budget, generally there is a heading for the communion of goods with members of the community who are in need. Only now, we were the ones in need. On the other hand our giving had always generated a constant stream of providence. As a consequence, one day one of our little ones, in a very decisive way announced, 'Yes, now I know what we must do: we have to give more.'

Basically, all of us felt that this was the right way; it would be living out the experience that this little one already knew. But to manage it we would have to cut something from the budget. And so we felt that we should no longer send our children to a fee-paying school, but to the State one, which was free. When we put this suggestion to our eldest boy, Ezekiel, who is six, he burst into tears and begged us to not make him change school, and he shut himself in his room.

As his mother, perhaps I was suffering more than he was, thinking of him suffering, but at the same time I felt I had to help him to make sense of this suffering, because only in this way could it be constructive. I went to his room and said to him, 'Look, your Mum's crying because she doesn't know what to do. Certainly the unknown is frightening. I don't know what this new school would be like, but new things open up new possibilities. You know, you have another mother, who is my

---

13. In the Gospel, Jesus says, 'Where two or three are gathered in my name, I am there among them.' (Mt. 18: 20).

mother too, Mary, who will look after you and will make sure that you don't have a bad time.'

While I was saying these things, I felt he was listening and at the end he hugged me tightly and, after a while said, 'Don't worry, Mum, I am happy. Why don't we go and look at the school?'

At that moment I had the impression that he had discovered who this other mother was and, perhaps, he had turned to her.

A few days went by. Every now and again the problem returned, but we remembered our situation and he was able to resign himself.

In the meantime Christmas came, and for a present his grandmother gave him precisely the right amount of money to pay the fees at the school where he went before. We, however, didn't have enough for the monthly bills.

The great surprise took place the next day. The school telephoned to say that that it had allocated a scholarship to Ezekiel because they did not want to lose a pupil who throughout the year had given so much to the others.

It was early in the morning and he was still sleeping. My husband and I couldn't wait any longer and we woke him and gave him the good news. He hugged me, as he had the time before, but without saying anything, as if absorbed in a private conversation.

I.A. and E. – Buenos Aires

Your Son is Like My Son

These days there isn't much work and it is clear that the situation isn't easy for anyone, myself included. There is little money at home and every day is a struggle.

In spite of this, because I believe that God loves us, beginning my day at work (in which every day is a struggle, not so much to increase the clientele, but to maintain the ones I have made over the years), I always try to see the positive in everything. This is one of the ways I have of loving each person I meet.

So it was one day when I went to visit a series of clients, amongst whom there was one in particular, whose business was on the point of collapse. He was in a very bad way.

We began to talk and it was natural for me to listen with special attention. I felt I had to take upon myself the burden of his lack of success, which inevitably weighs heavily on the father of a family, in these situations.

Through an intuition, which at times someone has and doesn't know how to explain, I felt that I had to do something so that he wouldn't remain in that state.

'It's right,' I said to him, 'everything you have told me is true. But that's not the only thing there is...' and I dared to suggest that he make an effort to consider what was positive in his life: his family, his children and many other things which I had noticed about him over these years of friendship.

In his eyes I read that such reasoning had made its mark: he was listening to me! But I didn't want it to end there. 'Look,' I said to him, 'I'll do the best I can to help you. I know that your son is looking for work. I may be able to do something for him.' And I had the feeling that my friend was a little comforted.

In reality, for some time I had planned to speak to a friend who worked for a multi-national company. He had said that there was a chance of some work for my son, who was also unemployed.

I met my friend and during the course of the conversation I asked if he could do anything for this trader's son.

Thinking about it, more recently, it was already a lot to ask for a job for one person, but for two…

'You see, this is important,' I explained. 'To be more precise it is so important that he should take preference over my son.'

I felt I must be honest and speak of the decision I had made instinctively faced with the desperation of this family. My son understood.

A few days later my friend from the multi-national company called to tell me that the young man he had introduced to the company, the trader's son, had come across very well in all his interviews and he had been chosen for the job.

The news filled me with joy and I told his father straight away. He didn't know how to thank me. He asked if we could meet immediately to celebrate and have a coffee together. He was radiant!

Our talk together went deeper and deeper. Towards the end he became very serious and he said to me, 'The day you came and helped me to see things more positively, I was in a very bad way. I had already decided to commit suicide. But after I had spoken with you I realized things were different, and so that I wouldn't fall into a similar temptation I threw my gun into the lake.'

M. V. – Buenos Aries

Size 47 Shoes

I found myself a few kilometres from Saō Paolo. Despite the fact that I was tired, the journey had gone very well. I was cheered by the fact that I'd managed to find a load to carry on the return journey. It wouldn't have been worth leaving Paranà to transport goods eight hundred kilometres as far as Saō Paolo without the guarantee of this other job on the return journey.

I had made my plans, and by the end of the week I would be back with the family! I needed to be with my children who feel it when their father isn't there. For my wife too, it was a special time because together we had lived through a difficult experience: I had wound up the partnership that I had had with my brothers in a joinery firm. I was one of the owners and worked in the firm's office. Because of a small disagreement among us, and so as not to break up our friendship and family ties, I had chosen to walk away. All I had left was a truck… but I was young and I had a family to support. With the support and encouragement of my wife, I began work as a truck driver. At the beginning it was very hard, I had to overcome my pride, but little by little I discovered the beauty and dignity of all work.

I made my delivery in good time and was in front of the firm where I was to pick up the new load. The gate-keeper who let me in eyed me from head to toe, finally settling on my sandals. The business did not allow drivers to drive in sandals. 'Unfortunately,' he told me, 'I'll have to give the load to someone else.' I couldn't believe it! We were in an isolated spot where there weren't any shops near by, and even if there had been any, it isn't easy to find a pair to fit me as I am tall and wear size 47! Almost desperate I explained the situation, but there was nothing to be done.

I returned to my truck deeply upset... all my plans had failed. By the time I'd found a new load for the return journey the end of the week would have gone.

I turned to Jesus: he knew that I wanted to be with my family.... Then Chiara's experience during the war, the one about the size 42 shoes, came to mind.[14] I too made the same request and with faith returned to the gatekeeper. To my surprise he looked at my feet and said, 'Go into that hut... there are lots of things, including shoes which have been left there for some time... they don't seem to belong to anyone... you never know what you might find!'

I rushed to the warehouse and... there they were, a new pair! I tried them on and they were just my size, 47. The joy I experienced was indescribable! Fresh proof that the Gospel is true!

J.L.C. – Paranà (Brazil)

---

14. See 'The First Time', p. 13.

The Founding of Mariapolis 'Life'

For some time we having been having quite a special adventure with a group of boys from the Movement. The group has a clear idea of 'nourishing ourselves with the Gospel to become a generation of saints', and we feel the need to meet often to help the boys develop and to find encouragement.

At one stage we had the idea of spending a weekend together in the countryside. Days went by, but we couldn't find the right place to go. At the last minute, one of our friends spoke of a nature centre, founded many years ago in the hills near Louvain. Visitors, especially young people, go there in great numbers, attracted by the quality of the air and by the unspoilt natural surroundings.

We went there and from the first moment of the weekend there was a great atmosphere among the boys, the organizers and Jean, the priest who went with us. We made a real competition of helping one another.

The programme included times when the boys could talk to Jean about matters of faith, but during the breaks they went to play in the woods.

So it was, that we came across an old man with the air of an elderly professor, who, leaning on his stick and accompanied by an enormous St Bernard, was walking calmly through the trees. The unknown person asked politely, 'Well lads, what interesting things have you done today?'

Without hesitation, one boy, not three feet in height, with a radiant face replied, 'We listened to lots of wonderful answers about Jesus' love for us.'

Another added that they had talked about the catechism. A third mentioned confession and the Eucharist. Having finished this brief conversation they ran off to continue playing.

Jean stayed a little longer with the elderly professor speaking of the beauty and hope of young people. He explained that the boys were, in a sense, the recent flowering of a great tree, one of the new movements in the Church called the Work of Mary.[15]

At these words the man's face lit up, but we could never have imagined what effect this meeting had on him.

A few weeks later there was a telephone call: the elderly man was none other than the celebrated Professor Paul Bouts, priest, scientist and founder of the centre where we had spent the weekend. 'For some time, as I said the rosary during my walks on the hillside, I confided in Mary my hope that all that I had achieved might be her work! Today I decided to leave as a legacy to you, the Work of Mary, all that I have built during my life, a wood of ten hectares, a youth centre with ninety beds, houses and buildings and a flourishing commercial enterprise …'

Jesus' promise came to mind immediately: 'Whoever has left [at least spiritually] houses, or brothers or sisters, father, mother, children or fields for my name, will receive a hundred times over.'

Today, on the hill where those children met with the professor, is the small town called Mariapolis 'Life'. It is

---

15. This is the name under which the Focolare Movement was approved by the Roman Catholic Church.

a centre for gospel witness and for the community life of the Focolare Movement in Belgium.

M. and O. – Brussels

Queuing Up For Water

I am Edine, a girl from Burundi.

One day there wasn't any water in the place where I live, and we had to go somewhere else to get it. There were lots of us, in a very long queue. Those who came from far away asked if they might go ahead of some people at the front, so that they could get home early, but no one would give way.

Sometime later a little boy with a bowl came along. He looked at me and asked if I would give my place to him. I did so straight away and felt a great joy in my heart.

Soon afterwards a woman arrived and said to us, 'As there are so many of you lining up to wait, some of you can come to my house for water.'

I felt it was God's reward.

E. – Burundi

A Thousand Dollars

We were preparing an event, which was to take place during the World Youth Day at Czestochowa.

To cover the cost of the hire of the sports ground where it was to take place, we agreed with the owner to pay part in dollars and part in brand-named sports articles.

Many of the young people brought to Czestochowa some excellent sports articles (tennis shoes, football boots, tracksuits etc.), given to us as sponsorship from Italian sports shops. We deposited these articles in the cellar in the school where we were staying. Next to it, in another store, we put used clothing, which had also been brought by the young people, only this was for the young people of the Eastern countries.

Each day I went past these two store-rooms: in the first I saw the richness of western Europe and in the other, old clothing, clean and well looked after, but used.

I couldn't accept that the old ones were for Jesus in the poor and the new ones to pay for the field, and therefore for ourselves. I felt like a hypocrite: how could we give old things to Jesus?

I consulted my friends, but everyone said that we didn't have the money to be able to give up this 'payment in kind' for the field. But I wasn't convinced. Every time I went there with one of the young people for used clothing, I felt bad.

Finally I had an idea: I could – with the faith that it had already been given – ask God for a thousand dollars, the value of the sports shoes and other items. In this way the new items wouldn't be needed to pay for the field, and they could be given to the poor.

As soon as I'd worked out this solution, a Romanian youth asked for a pair of shoes for another boy. I went to the first store and asked how many of them there were.

'There are two coach loads of us.'

'Choose what you need,' I replied.

The youth couldn't believe his eyes. He was drawn particularly to the football boots for smaller boys. Before he left in the coach full of things, he confided, 'I went to church and I asked the Eternal Father for a pair of boots for one boy who didn't have any, but I didn't dare to ask for the others. And look what God has done!'

The next day I received the thousand dollars!

U.B. – Castelli Romani (Italy)

The World Will Change

One day in September I left for a town four hours away from Bogotá, to make a delivery for the printer's where I work. I delivered the parcel and went to the bus station. While I was waiting for the bus to leave, I was approached by a young guy, who talked to me in a friendly way. At one point he asked me about the current situation in Colombia. I answered that Colombia and the world are suffering from violence because people don't love one another, and don't live in unity.

'But what is unity?' he asked me.

I replied, 'Unity is the only power capable of changing the world

I then told him something about my life as a Christian.

He listened with interest. I noticed that even though he seemed decent, there was something troubling him.

When it was time to get on the bus I said 'goodbye' to him, since he had told me he had come simply to send a package.

The bus was just about to go when the police arrived. They asked us all to get off so that they could search the bus and the passengers. The police targeted me particularly and questioned me thoroughly. I was very frightened and hundreds of thoughts went through my head. I asked Jesus to help me from that moment, as he knew I hadn't done anything wrong.

After twenty minutes of interrogation, one of the policemen changed his attitude towards me. Showing me some wrappings containing dynamite, he told me that a little earlier he had received an anonymous telephone call informing him that the caller had been paid to place a bomb on the bus. However, having met someone among the passengers who had talked to him of new hope for the world, and who had made him feel the joy of life for just a moment, he thought that life was worth more than anything else, and so he had decided to call the police to warn them to remove the parcel from the bus and to defuse the dynamite.

He added that he was not someone who believed in God, but he hoped and prayed that the massacre could be stopped in time. He also asked that they look for a young man in a white shirt with a blue jacket and tell him that with his answers and his attitude, he would certainly help to save the world, as today he had saved him. Then abruptly he had hung up the telephone.

I took a deep breath, and finding myself once more on the bus for home, thought that by now I could have been dead. I said to myself, however, that if that had happened, I would have died in the certainty that the world will change.

J.G.B. – Colombia

The Fatherhood of God

I live in Rio Grande, a city in the state of Rio Grande South, and I have been married for more than twenty-five years. When I was pregnant with my fourth daughter, we were living in a small house where there was no room for another bed. I was feeling very apprehensive and frightened for the future, particularly because our financial situation was very shaky. Faith, however, told me not to worry, but to cast all my cares into the Father's heart, who cares even for the birds of the air...

My husband, Celso, and I reminded ourselves that in the Gospel, Jesus says that whatever we ask for, united in his name, he will give, and so that's what we did.

A few days later, one of our neighbours, who knew about my pregnancy, came bringing some things for me that had belonged to her grandchild. There was even a cot and a mattress. It was the answer.

Following this, keeping faithful to the will of God and offering to him with patience all the disapproval among family and friends every time we had a baby, we have always felt God's fatherhood, who in a thousand different ways has looked after our needs. So it was for our other three children, and for the building improvements... Now our older children have started to go to work, but truly we have never wanted for anything.

L.F. – Rio Grande (Brazil)

The Last Address

The task of finding part-time work, as required by my job in our little town in Montet, seemed almost impossible. I had arrived only two weeks earlier with scant knowledge of the language.

I searched systematically and unceasingly, but to no avail.

One morning I left the focolare saying, 'Today I'm going to find it!' because the next day I had to leave to prepare for the summer Mariapolis.

With the last address in my hand, I headed for a church and went inside. I cast my worry into the heart of God, certain that he would take care of it, and I asked him to fill my small heart with a greater and more radical love and to be faithful to him and his will.

Feeling free and happy, I went to the remaining address. The personnel manager, after listening to my request, looked at me with surprise and said, 'Who gave you my address? You're just the person I was looking for.'

R.O. – *Montet (Switzerland)*

He Felt Love

During my shift I received an urgent call from the Intensive Care ward, where there was a fifty-two year-old man, who had been admitted following a serious injury to his eyes. He was not moving in his bed and seemed to be apathetic. I asked for some information and was told that he had been shot in the head. His brain, however, was uninjured. While he was asking for a lethal injection, I realized that his soul as well as his body was sick. I needed to be very patient and try to understand him.

Throughout my visit he asked continually for an injection because he wanted to die.

The operation was complicated and lasted until night-time. It wasn't possible to save one of his eyes, and the other was badly damaged. He stayed in intensive care for a week.

Every day I asked about his condition and together with a friend prayed with faith for him. He was brought to my ward. Throughout the day there was a lot of work to do, but before going home I stopped to greet him. Beside his bed I asked him, 'Do you know who I am?'

He answered straight away, 'I can't see, but I think you're the doctor who operated on me. During the operation I felt a great love.'

I promised him that I would do all that I could to save his eye, without being absolutely certain that I would be able to do so. One morning, however, almost by miracle, the patient said that he could see some light. Every day his sight improved, until it was completely restored. The eye was saved!

After a few months he came to thank me and he told me that once more he had found the path to God. His marriage was back on track, and he was very happy with only one eye.

Joking, I said to him that he needed to lose an eye to see better.

E.S. – Italy

Continual Providence from God

Edward and Carmen are husband and wife. In one of the Movement's meetings Edward said, 'We are a poor family with three small children and at one time I was without work. For some time there had been a battle going on inside me, but I didn't have the courage to start a new life. I understood that to help me, God was asking for a radical conversion.

'One day, almost desperate because my little girls had nothing to eat and didn't have any shoes to go to school, I went into a church and in tears knelt down and asked forgiveness from God for everything, and requested the possibility of work.

'That was on Friday, and by Monday I had a job. That's when I understood how much God loves me and that he had forgiven me and helped me: God's love and mercy are greater than our sins!

'And so began a new phase in our family. My wife and children taught me Gospel love, which they had learned and I, too, tried to live the same way.

'In the meantime I was astonished by the way God's providence started to arrive in abundance. I was so taken aback that at times I cried because I was so moved.

'On one occasion when my children were on their own at home, someone came to ask for some sugar. Without hesitation they took all that there was and gave it. After a moment's hesitation, my wife said to the children, "Perhaps this person needed it more than we did. What matters is to give this sugar from the heart. Jesus will think of us."

'In fact, soon after there was a knock on the door. It was another person who had brought us a bag of groceries, amongst which was some sugar, double the amount given away.'

Carmen continued, 'With Edward's first earnings we were able to buy a pair of shoes for one of our little girls. One day she came home from school and said to me, "Mum, I've noticed that one of my friends has shoes that are badly worn and so I'd like to give her mine," and she added, 'You have taught us that when we give something to someone, we have to give them the best, and so I'd like to give her my new shoes.'

'I was taken aback, I didn't know what to say. On the one hand what my daughter said was true, but on the other hand, I knew how much the shoes had cost. In the end, together we decided to give them.

'Three days later, a third person came to the door saying that she had just bought a pair of shoes for her daughter, but they were too small. So, she had brought them to us in case we needed them. They were the same size as those of my daughter.

'One evening we went to visit some relatives whose children were eating bread and cooked ham for supper. As we left, our children wanted the same kind of sandwiches as theirs. I said no because we had only enough money for the next day's lunch. But they insisted, saying that surely Jesus would pay me back. They convinced me and I gave it to them, only that the next day, when I had to do the shopping, I didn't have any money. But the children were ready with an answer, 'You'll see Jesus won't be long in sending it.'

'A few minutes later there was a knock on the door. It was a fourth person who had owed me money for some time. She had brought the exact amount of money that I had spent earlier.'

E. and C. – Puebla (Mexico)

A Grace Received

I wasn't able to admit that I was ill with alcoholism. On the other hand I was ashamed of not being able to resist alcohol, but rejected all help from other people. With this growing unease I implored God to grant me a grace.

After a morning in a furniture warehouse, I began a personal, very open and deep conversation with a friend. It wasn't simply a chat, but a demanding exchange with some very difficult moments: very salutary. My friend offered me whatever support I needed so long as I decided to get over this illness.

Fully facing up to my situation and admitting my weakness had, in a way, freed me.

I felt I was sinking into nothing, but at the same time I was sure of God's love, to whom I had entrusted myself, and of my friend's love too. I felt the strength to go for a radical treatment plan covering all aspects: medical, psychological and spiritual. The way forward would be demanding and difficult.

Little by little my sense of isolation disappeared. I experienced forgiveness and I, too, was able to forgive. I was able to be sincere and to acquire the right kind of humility, recognizing my errors and defects. At one point I managed to give up my own limited goals and plans and abandoned myself to God's plans, choosing

Jesus crucified as my only good, as I had never done before.[16]

It seemed like the ticket to a new life.

Now I live with a very special joy, like a person who has been born again. Although at work alcohol is only a hand's breadth away, it has been more than a year and a half since I have had a relapse. The doctors are amazed and consider me a miracle. I see it as a grace received.

X.E. – Austria

The Hundredfold[17]

At the office I had put in an application to receive financial help for the planning costs of a house I was building as part of a co-operative. It was the sort of thing where you apply and then... In the meantime Christmas was approaching and that year as building costs had absorbed most of our savings, unlike other years, we didn't go to relatives who live some distance away.

At the same time we received a telephone call from a close friend who proposed that we club together to send some money for Biafra. The situation there was deteriorating, especially for children. In the family we were thinking about next Christmas, with its expenses, pres-

---

16. An arrow prayer common to members of the Movement is, 'You, Lord, are my only good'. (cf. Ps.16[15]:2).
17. The reference is to the hundredfold given to those who renounce goods and relationships for the sake of the Gospel, referred to in Mt 19:29 and Mk 10:30, cf. also Lk 18:29-30.

ents, food… and since we already shared our surplus in various ways with our community we felt a bit concerned. But we felt certain of God's providence and so we did not let ourselves hesitate at all and sent everything we could give, fifty thousand lire.

A few days went by and I received a telephone call from the office. Someone informed me that I had been awarded the sum of five million lire as a non-returnable payment for the planning costs.

I worked out the figures. We had given away fifty thousand lire to Biafra and a hundred times that amount had arrived. 'Impressive,' I exclaimed, 'how mathematically exact the Gospel is!'[18]

F.G. - Italy

A Mother Who is Beautiful Too

We are a group of friends who often meet together. One particular evening, one of us wasn't there. We discovered that she was expecting a baby and that her boyfriend, who had decided to leave her, was doing all that he could to convince her to have an abortion.

Her parents too, who were poor and had bad social problems, didn't want anything to do with the baby. Neither did her closest relatives.

Weak and confused, she didn't know how to react to the pressure. Only when she was with us was she able to

---

18. The reference is to the hundredfold referred to in Mt 19:29 and Mk 10:30, cf. also Lk 18:29-30.

talk about this decision, but then when she returned home her family's insistence and her financial circumstances convinced her to go for an abortion.

She decided. She booked an appointment for a consultation and for the procedure itself.

In the meantime we did everything we could: we prayed, went for walks with her, visited her family, contacted the 'Movement For Life' and managed to find some financial help…

On the evening of 10 May, Mother's Day, we invited her for supper at one of our houses, together with all the young men and women who form part of our group.

At the end we said that next year she would have the 'lead role' when it came to celebrating Mother's Day.

It was an emotional moment for us all, but by that point it was too late. The appointment was in a few days' time. There was nothing else to be done.

We didn't give up hope because we knew that if we prayed united in the name of Jesus 'mountains would move' and so on the eve of the procedure we met together in this way, to ask for a miracle: to save the life of the little child.

The next day as a huge act of love, we went to help her and take her to the hospital. She saw us, took a deep breath and said to us, 'Are you going to give me a lift to the hairdresser's? You know, a good mother must be beautiful too.'

M.T. – Palermo

Double the Amount of Providence

With the certainty that the Lord loves us and takes care of us, we were looking for a new apartment, because the focolare house where we lived was too small for six of us. We had looked through lots of advertisements in the newspapers... in vain. It seemed like an impossible task. At one stage we were offered a flat on the ground floor, and although we were a bit concerned for our security (we are all women), we thought we would take it, but would close off the portico that ran along the side. The council, however, would not grant permission for this, as it was a building of architectural importance and was protected by law. Given the continual difficulties we were rethinking whether to take the risk when one of the focolarine, Jolante, met a woman on the bus who began talking to her. The focolarina listened to her with love: it was Jesus! Getting off at the same stop, the woman, perhaps because she felt loved, opened her heart to Jolanta. For months she had been trying to sell her apartment, but without success.

Jolante told us about all about it and we went to see the apartment, which cost less than the other. It was on the third floor, full of light and was spacious: truly God's providence... And this seemed even clearer to us when we heard that, at the same time as this was going, there had been a robbery at the ground floor flat. The burglars, who managed to break in without a problem, stole everything. We thanked the Lord twice over!

C. – Vilnius (Lithuania)

If God Is With Us ...

An appointment to buy the land for the Movement's little town in France was arranged for 10 o'clock in the morning.

Six of us met up at the underground station. Before meeting with the notary we spent a moment deciding what each of us was to do.

We declared our fullest unity with one another,[19] conscious of the enormity of the responsibility we were taking on, which would involve the whole of the Movement in France and would mark an important stage in our journey. We went with butterflies in our stomachs, a good dose of the fear of God, and a tremendous trust in him.

Chiara was with us spiritually. A telephone call, which we had received the day before, confirmed this: 'Go ahead in the certainty that ours is a work of God.'

How else could it have been, when the capital raised in approximately ten years was the fruit of gifts, great and small, from innumerable people?

People who had sacrificed a birthday present, changing their car, a piece of jewellery, a dress or their annual bonus: all were small or not so small acts of love, known more often than not only to God.

We went towards the office and, 'Look,' said one of us astonished. At the corner of the street, right in the centre of Paris there was a parked lorry with: 'If God is with us, who can be against us?' painted on it.

---

19. Unity means complete agreement in thought and heart.

You cannot imagine all the obstacles our team had to face during the six hours of very difficult negotiations. As a background, however, were those words full of light echoing in our hearts: 'If God is with us, who can be against us?'

Finally we reached an agreement and signed the document.

D.B. - France

The Gospel's Revolution is Infectious

After I finished University (I had been married for a year) we had our first children, twin boys: Peter and Simon. Eighteen months later Elizabeth was born and after another eighteen months, Monica. It seemed obvious to my husband and me that I wouldn't look for a job, but I would stay at home to give the children the security and warmth of a family. Later, after two and three years respectively, Matthew and Anna came along.

In seven years we were a family of eight and for more than fifteen years we lived on my husband's salary. Throughout those years we never wanted for anything. Quite the opposite, we were able to give our surplus to others.

We had difficulties at times, but we did not worry because providence always came along almost before we needed it.

The most important thing for us was to look for the kingdom of God, which meant to keep alive our love for one another and for others. And God will not be outdone in generosity...

If at lunch we had eaten the last of our potatoes, by four o'clock one of our friends would come to the door to ask if we needed any... potatoes.

If on a Monday we took a bag of children's clothes, which we didn't need any more, to the focolare, the following Friday we would receive two bags containing things we did need. And our children absorbed this way of thinking.

'Give and it will be given,' became the law of their lives.

When some of their friends came round to play, there was a competition: 'Can we give this toy to Andrew?'

'Of course!'

One friend was being confirmed. He didn't have a watch. Simon had received a lovely watch from his grandparents and was happy to give it away.

When the children started to go to school we needed a good big table. We looked for a joiner to come round to take the measurements. After a week he came back with a wonderful table. He set it up and gave it to us for nothing. All he wanted was for us to remain friends.

Our neighbours would ask us, 'But how do you do it? Your children are better dressed than ours.'

We told them about our way of life and they wanted to do the same thing.

One day we received the money to buy a new minibus from a person we didn't know and so on the day of our wedding anniversary it was already there. For the first trip out we invited all the children in our building. Happiness was everywhere. It felt as if we were travelling in the love of God.

A family from former Yugoslavia

Algeria, the Festival of Eid

It was a few days before Eid, the Muslim festival when the sacrifice of Abraham is remembered. Each family sacrifices a sheep and shares it with those who can't afford to do the same.

A friend confided in us, 'I work as a social worker in a school. We received funds to buy clothing for more than a hundred children in a very poor area. Unfortunately, there wasn't enough to buy them any meat for the festival. But they couldn't go without this, surely!'

We had only just returned home when we received a telephone call, 'For the festival we'd like to share our meat with someone, can you help?'

It was the equivalent of two sheep.

Having made contact between the person offering the meat and the person who asked for it, we then had to cut it, weigh it and package it...

Our focolare kitchen was transformed and in a few hours everything was ready. Not one of the hundred families would go without meat, everyone had at least a little.

On the same day we informed our Muslim friends of a need that we had only just heard about.

In a public maternity clinic, many children had been left abandoned. No funds had been allocated; it was almost as if these children didn't exist either for the State or for their parents, or even for their mothers who had been forced into taking such a desperate action.

Everything was missing, from milk to cots to lie in. Such milk as there was, the staff paid for out of their own money.

Among those to whom we had mentioned this, one woman did not hesitate to say, 'Haven't you got any milk? I'll bring you a good supply of it tomorrow.' And that's what happened.

Talking about these small experiences brought about a chain reaction, those who could offer something on the one hand, and the discovery of those in need on the other.

And we are there in the middle of it all. It's a question of building a bridge, which unites.

MT.S. - Algeria

An E-mail from God

Nico had been in the focolare in Vilnius for almost two years. After taking a four month course in Lithuanian – a linguistic maze because of the enormous number of declensions and exceptions to the rules – he saw that it that it wasn't going to be possible to take a further, advanced course because of the amount of work that needed to be done for the Movement, which was growing fast.

In the post-communist era, where the State needed to be completely rebuilt, legislation was in a constant state of flux. One day Nico suddenly realized that the Movement's legal status was no longer recognized, without anyone being aware of it. It seemed that the apartments and some of the cars, registered to the Movement, could be seized by the State. Not only this, Nico discovered that according to the new law the Movement would now be considered 'profit-making', which meant that it could be liable to assessment by the tax office. This was a problem, since as a result of frequently having had to move house, very few invoices had been kept.

Nico made hundreds of visits to the Tax Office, to the Ministry of Justice, the Ministry of Finance, and to the Diocesan Curia. He tried to explain the problem as well as a Dutchman could in a difficult language.

The situation was anything but happy. Every employee said something different from his colleague, and each one was convinced he was right.

Who to ask for advice? Friends abroad? What could they do other than worry?

These came a point when even a woman friend, who was employed at the Tax Office, said that it was necessary to pay 20% on all the financial help received from abroad for the past five years: a substantial sum of money.

Going home with this latest news, Nico said in his heart, as if speaking to God: 'I want to believe in your love, but sometimes you play Hide and Seek!'

As soon as he arrived home, the doorbell rang. It was a young man who was looking for a bit of company. It wasn't exactly the right moment for Nico to have a chat in Lithuanian, but it was Jesus and he needed to be loved.

When the young man left, Nico opened his electronic mail and found a short message from his friend, Hans.

'Dear Nico, you've come to mind quite often recently and I wanted to assure you of my unity.'

There was nothing more.

But, between the lines he seemed to read, 'You'll see, Nico, everything will be all right. I am with you.'

A few days later he met a Member of Parliament who was a lawyer, who, in a very short space of time, set everything to rights.

Nico receives a lot of e-mails, but the one from Hans, which was only a greeting, a sign of brotherly love, seemed like an e-mail from God.

N.T. – Vilnius (Lithuania)

Because of an Act of Love

While I was on a daily walk as directed by my doctor, I was trying to get to know the area where I had been living for a short time. I was the new bishop.

A few days later, I started to tidy up a few things in the bishop's house, so that it would better express God, who is beauty. I found some bronze candelabras, which didn't really fit in.

A small shop selling second-hand goods, which I had seen on my walk, came to mind. I thought that given the tough economic conditions in the country, the owner might be in serious difficulties.

I asked my secretary to parcel up the candelabras and give them to the shopkeeper with a card, which read: 'I am a little gift from the bishop. If you manage to sell this, please give the money to the poor. But if you need it for yourself, you can keep it.'

Unexpectedly, during the afternoon the man came to the bishop's house. He insisted on seeing me. When I met him he said to me, 'Today I wanted to commit suicide, but when your secretary came, I realized that someone still cared for me, and I changed my mind. Many thanks!'

R., Bishop – Argentina

An Inspection Lasting Four Months

One day I went to inspect a company accused on many counts of breaking the law, such as by paying unjust wages, demanding staff work at weekends and unpaid overtime...

As soon as I arrived, the owner took me to one side, thinking that I was more interested in receiving money than in carrying out an inspection. When he realized I was serious about my job, he changed his attitude immediately and spoke aggressively, telling me that he would determine the law in his company, that I could give him as many fines as I liked, but he wouldn't change anything, and even though he knew that I would persist, he was unafraid.

Entrusting myself to Jesus, I felt the courage and strength to be calm and steady in purpose, even if I felt shattered. I wrote out the official statement of the company's breaches of the law while he became more and more hostile.

I had to return two, three, four times. And each time was an effort because I knew I was not welcome there... quite the opposite! The inspection dragged on for four months until eventually the people of the company began to realize that I was not doing this simply because I wanted to apply the law, but it was out of love for others, for the company's employees, who needed me to do what I did.

They then began to take my directives seriously and implemented them.

A few days ago I met the owner's son, who made a big fuss of me, asking when I was going back to carry out a new inspection! Another day his father called out to me in the street, 'I saw you from a distance and wanted to say hello.' He looked calm and full of gratitude!

MDR. F.C. – Brazil

Workers for his Vineyard

I was worried because one year, only two potential focolarine would be going to the formation school at Mariapolis Ginetta,[20] whereas in past years there had been a minimum of four. I said a complete yes to God. I put this worry into the Father's heart, and together with my focolare each day I prayed for 'workers' for his vineyard. I didn't have to wait long for his answer. Another five young people went in February and four or five will go in June and at the end of the year – it's incredible – another twenty-nine potential focolarine are getting ready to go.

How can I doubt God's love?

G.C. – Belém (Brazil)

---

20. This is the name of the Focolare little town in Brazil dedicated to Ginetta Calliari – now in the next life – who founded it and built it.

Our Small Hall

Each year, when we young people finish our time at Mariapolis Ginetta in Brazil, having experienced a life of unity there, we leave for home and others come to take part in the same 'school'. At the school we have lessons, times when we meet and share, periods when we rest and other activities that we do. We even prepare a musical show. The area where we put on the show, however, at one point was becoming far too small. We had to sit on the floor and weren't able to move while the show was on. We asked the Eternal Father to help us build a small hall.

In past years, we knew that other young people had made sacrifices, given things up and raised funds precisely for this, but every time they had almost reached the amount needed, they gave it away to meet another of the little town's needs. This year, after several months' effort, we had almost enough. But, yet again, unexpectedly, immediate help was needed elsewhere. How could we not be open to others? And so, once again, we gave it all away.

One day a focolarina, on her way to Italy, used the occasion to visit some of our friends who had helped out in the past. As usual, she laid out plans for some projects for the little town, on the table. One of these friends, who was a builder, gave them a quick look over. Then, he pointed at one project in particular, our small hall. 'I'd like to help with this,' he said.

Young people from Mariapolis Ginetta – Brazil

He Will Take Care of Us

For very many years Chiara has been living with faith the Word of God: 'Cast all your anxieties on him, because he cares for you' (cf. 1 Pt. 5:7) and she assures us that on the innumerable occasions when she has put it into practice, never has she been let down.

This is one example among many.

One day, the hospital bill for a focolarina's operation arrived. It was for a hundred million lire.

To tell you the truth, at first she was shocked... but as ever, she entrusted this worry to God's providence.

About that time an adherent received a legacy.

She gave the house to her children, and what she received in liquid assetsz to Chiara. It was exactly a hundred million!

D.Z. – Rocca di Papa (Rome)

Landing in the Mountains in Cameroon

On the 4 May 2000, Chiara was expected in Fontem, a village lost in a tropical forest in Cameroon.

She was to have landed by helicopter at Belleh, a village very close to Fontem. When the expected time for her arrival came, there was no sound of a helicopter, nor in the hours that followed, and people began to get worried.

After long attempts by satellite telephone, the only means of communication, news came that the helicopter had set off on time from Douala but it hadn't arrived at Fontem.

Everyone waited in suspense, until three hours later there came a communication from a radio operator that Chiara, and those travelling with her, were about to arrive by Land Rover!

Because of thick fog, the helicopter hadn't been able to reach Fontem, but had been forced to land at Fongutongu, a place lost on the mountains in the forest twenty-four kilometres from Fontem. As they got out into the burning sun, they had seen African boys and girls popping up all around. The pilot managed to keep them at a distance using pallets and some rope.

Chiara smiled at the children and prayed with the others quite calmly. Lucio, who was with her, approached one of the men who lived there, who would happily have taken them to their destination, but he didn't have any petrol for his lorry. And so he went and sat at the side of the road to see if someone passing by could notify Fontem so they could be collected by Land Rover.

And now there was a tangible sign of God's love.

Only three minutes had gone by when a car approached.

It was Bishop Agostino Delfino, a friend of the Movement, who having come from the Central African Republic, after a two-day journey, was passing at exactly that moment and was going in the same direction. Delighted, he drove Chiara and the others to Fontem and everyone's heart was bursting with joy.

And that stay at Fongutongu had not been in vain, since the people there, getting to know what Chiara and the others were going to do in Fontem, wanted to know about the spirituality, so that they too could live it.

A.P.M. - Rome

Mary's Crown

As there are more than twenty of our little towns that witness the Gospel, we wanted to have one here in Holland. We looked at various pieces of land, but none of them were suitable because of the buildings already there. Chiara advised us to look for land without buildings.

Since in Holland, as we say, on every handkerchief of land there are at least two cows, as it is nearly all agricultural, we had no option but to look in the 'polders', land reclaimed from the sea. In fact we found some land at Almere, and we had drawn up some plans with an architect and started proceedings with the local council. However, every time we spoke to Chiara, she said, 'Aren't you worried that the water might come back?'

Each time we replied that the safety dykes would prevent this. However, as we were struck by Chiara's insistence, we asked Our Lady, in the church of the Sweet Mother,[21] typical of our country, to give us a sign. We suggested that, for example, someone could give us some land elsewhere, even though we were well aware that no one had any land where construction was allowed. But Someone knew of a place!

---

21. The name under which Our Lady is venerated in Holland at Hertogenbosch.

A few days before we signed the papers to buy the land at Almere (which would have cost all the money we had been able to scrape together up to that point), while we were in the Council buildings, we heard about a bishop who had a Cistercian abbey in his diocese that was about to close. It was called Marienkroon, that is, 'Crown of Mary'. It was surrounded by a good bit of land on which it was possible to build.

Having remembered that we were looking for land for our little town, the bishop let us know about it. We went to see it: it seemed like the answer from the Sweet Mother. We were delighted.

Furthermore, about this time, a newspaper announced in an article that the State could no longer guarantee that the land at Almere would remain dry, because part of it was sinking and the water table was rising: it was just in time to stop us throwing all our money, which had been collected with great sacrifice, 'into the water', but we could now use it to build on the new land. Perhaps the Sweet Mother wanted us next to her, as a little crown, to honour her.

L.S. – Holland

The Robbers' Excuses

We are ten teenage girls from different states in Brazil, who have come together for a year to deepen our understanding of the Focolare Movement's spirituality at Mariapolis Ginetta near Saõ Paolo.

One evening, straight after supper, two men came into the house. One of them wore a hood and had a revolver. They pushed us into the kitchen and lined us up with our faces to the wall. They wanted our money. The focolarina who was with us explained that we were students and didn't have money or jewellery, but that we would give them all we had. While she went to get her bag, one of us asked the robber, 'May we pray?'

There was no reply except for a rough gesture that we turn towards the wall.

She was insistent, asking the question two, three, four times.

Eventually, when they said yes, we prayed to Our Lady, in a loud voice, saying one Hail Mary after another.

When the robbers saw the little pile of low denomination bank notes, they took some of them and left the rest. They wanted to see the house, and following behind them, we said that we could understand the difficulties they had which made them act that way and that we would pray for them.

After they had told us to stay in the house and not to tell anyone, they went. At the door, turning round to us they asked pardon of us.

We found ourselves in the hall, silent, looking at one another with fear in our hearts and in our eyes, and with the certainty that Our Lady had saved us.

The Gospel from that morning's mass came to mind: 'You will be hated by all because of my name. But not a hair of your head will perish' (Lk 21: 17-18).

We were very much aware that the robbers hadn't even realized that we were all girls and that they could have done us real harm.

We then realized that we had all had the same thought: 'If by chance the robbers need hostages, I'll be the first to go,' because if, throughout the year, each morning we had made a pact to give our lives for one another, perhaps the moment had come to do it for real.

Young women from Mariapolis Ginetta - Brazil

They Spoke of a Miracle

The Consortium of Tassano Co-operatives at Sestri Levante had to find some new premises to house its many activities, which employ large numbers of disadvantaged people. Their current building was due for demolition. To build a new one would cost several million lire, and there wasn't enough money.

The president of the Consortium and his members prayed with faith, convinced that God's providence would intervene.

Although at the beginning of the initiative help had come from the unity of all the Catholic Movements in the diocese, now it would have to come from the various political and social bodies in the region. Applications were made to the Council and to the Regional Authority.

From the very beginning, in social and political meetings, there were various difficulties, but the stake-holders continued to believe.

At the same time the witness of unity, shown by the stake-holders of Tassano Co-operatives, had impressed the regional authorities so much so that one of their members had seen it as an example of how politics should be conducted: majority and minority parties working together without division.

In the end the regional authorities agreed to take upon themselves the total cost for what was necessary: approximately six billion lire. One mayor spoke of the miracle of providence.

F.l. - Liguria

Baby Jesus

In Venezuela after the great flood in which thousands of people were made homeless, people who belonged to the Movement often went to a reception centre for the victims. On Christmas Day we went there with our children, who at that time customarily give little statues of the baby Jesus to passers by, as a reminder of the significance of Christmas. Among others they saw a man with three children, whose wife was missing because of the floods. He was very sad and worried.

One of our children offered him a little statue. He took the Baby Jesus and with the others asked for a miracle: to find his wife.

The next day the man rushed towards the children, gestured towards the Baby Jesus and said, 'It was him: he brought about the miracle.' He had found his wife.

MA. DT. – Venezuela

Handed Back to her Mother

It was a hard and difficult time in Rwanda, typical of the aftermath of war. All the different offices and international agencies were beginning to take stock of the situation by gathering together statistics, and opening registries etc.

I was at work and I was registering some orphans' names.

At a certain point my heart missed a beat: among the many names, I saw one, which I recognized. Yes, it was my niece, my sister's daughter, who we thought had died with the others. She was only fourteen years old.

If, to say the least, I was saddened before, now I was really desperate. There was absolutely nothing I could do: if I admitted the situation, I would have put her in danger of her life. The fact was she was in the Congo, in a refugee camp with other tribes. If by chance they discovered the girl was from our tribe, they would kill her. I found myself with my hands tied.

I talked to trustworthy people who could perhaps do something. Together we looked at various solutions but in this case there didn't seem to be one. I was prey to dismay and discouragement.

All of a sudden, after several sleepless nights, I felt crowding into my mind Jesus' words, such as, 'Ask and you will receive'; 'What is impossible to man is possible to God'; 'With faith you can move mountains'…

'Here is the solution,' I said to myself. I rushed into the little church and in front of Jesus, I said to him, 'Jesus, Christmas is almost here and I have come to ask you for a gift. I ask that during the Christmas period my niece might come home. I don't know how or when, but you know.'

After a short time I received a telephone call. It was my sister: 'Your niece is home safe and sound.'

Miraculously she managed to escape from the refugee camp and reached the border between Rwanda and the Congo on foot.

She asked help of the soldiers and they brought her home and handed her back to her mother.

X.X. – Rwanda

Zero Sum

Since 1980, Chiara has been holding a monthly conference call with those in charge of the Movement in the various parts of the world. She links up with thousands of people in 91 cities all over the planet, who in their turn are linked with another 249 cities.

Wishing to advance the Kingdom of God wherever the Movement is present, Chiara communicates an important thought drawn from the spirituality of unity in order to maintain a high temperature of love for God and neighbour among everyone. After Chiara has spoken, one of her first companions and a young focolarino report on the most important things that have happened in the Movement during the preceding weeks.

The Swiss telephone company Swisscom is used to make the conference calls, which create a deep universal communion. Each month the bill arrives specifying the numbers of those who have been connected and the cost and the duration of each individual line.

The cost is high, but it has never been a burden to the Centre of the Movement because spontaneously people from all over give money so that this activity can continue.

Something a little different happened last year, though.

From December 2000, despite repeated attempts from the telephonists at Swisscom, all of them Swiss and therefore very organized, it has been impossible to make their computer work, so the computer that links to Chiara and the other two speakers on her line won't register the cost of the telephone call. The numbers, minutes and cost of all the zones in the world, which are linked, appear on the monthly bill. The line, connecting Chiara and the other two speakers with her, registers the number of the telephone and the duration of the call, as with all the other lines, whereas in the place where the cost should appear '00.00' is registered. And this happens not just to that one line, but with all the lines where someone actually says something.

Could this be a computer age gift of providence in response to having spread the Kingdom of God?

A.P.M. – Rocca di Papa (Rome)

My Yes

Half way through May in 1957, I began to have of a bad pain in my back and in my leg. It was so bad that I couldn't walk and had to stay in bed. The doctor who saw me wasn't able to make a diagnosis; it could have been sciatica or a slipped disc or something else. He decided to send me for X-rays.

Each day the pain grew worse and painkillers weren't able to relieve it. I waited anxiously for the results of the X-rays in the hope of finding the cause and therefore the cure.

On my bedside table I had a little picture of Jesus crucified and forsaken,[22] which reminded me of the choice I had made ten year earlier: to have him as the ideal of my life. I had a continuous dialogue with him and I forced myself to offer to him what I was suffering.

Eventually, the results of the X-rays arrived: decalcification of the bone! I asked my doctor what this illness meant. Decalcification of the bone meant that I would become progressively incapable of moving, it meant that I would end up in a wheelchair.

It was a moment of bewilderment. I wasn't yet thirty years old and before me was the prospect of a short life, full of suffering, and even more I would be a burden for whoever had to look after me.

My gaze rested on that picture of Jesus crucified and forsaken and I gave him my yes with the decision to accept the situation completely. Straight away I felt the joy of having been able to give him something.

The pain, however, began to lessen and after a month I had more X-rays at another clinic. The results were truly surprising. The radiologist assured me that she had rarely seen bone density so perfect and that undoubtedly the earlier X-rays had been done badly or could even have belonged to someone else.

I am now seventy-six and am still working!

M.T. – Rocca di Papa (Rome)

---

22. An image much loved by members of the Movement.

Alive by Miracle

I am a focolarina. I was in Rome for a professional course and at the end of the day I was at Stazione Termini (the train terminus). While I was waiting for a train to Frascati, I saw a crowd of frightened people crying out.

From where I was, I could see a body, which wasn't moving, between the railway lines.

I ran straight away to the body, it was someone who had been hit by a train, and knelt down. Lots of people were shouting not to touch, but I am a nurse, so I went ahead, took the coat off her face and found it was a girl. The situation was critical. I asked someone to call an ambulance and in the meantime I tried to resuscitate her: she might still be alive. The train had cut off her left leg and she was losing a lot of blood. I asked a man for his belt and stopped the bleeding. The girl had even more injuries, a head injury and her remaining leg was broken in several places.

I realized she was responding to what I was doing. Making her breathe rhythmically, I tried to calm her, giving her comfort and security.

After fifteen minutes she began to go into shock because of the loss of blood, and I feared she would not survive.

But her face full of blood, covered by long hair, reminded me of Jesus crucified. I concentrated and asked him to save her or to take her straight to heaven. I don't know what happened, but I felt a great heat in my hands and I saw both the girl, and myself enveloped in a great light. I no longer heard the voices around me;

everything was still. I had the impression that Someone 'invisible' was there. I felt a great peace, a deep, extraordinary relationship with Jesus.

The ambulance's siren recalled me to the cold facts of the situation. The doctor, faced with this extremely critical situation, was at a loss what to do, and the ambulance personnel stood by waiting for instructions. I introduced myself as a nurse and suggested what should be done. What amazed me was with what strength I took the situation in hand, as if it was Jesus in me who was doing it. I found myself directing operations and, to my surprise, they all obeyed.

We were able to save the girl without any further complications.

Then I took the train for Frascati. During the journey a woman recognized me, 'But you are the one who saved the girl! I was struck by how you acted in this tragedy: you seemed like an angel.'

A colleague on a course I was on worked in the intensive care unit where the girl was taken after her operation. She telephoned to tell me of her amazement, and that of the doctors: the girl was alive by miracle and it was providential for her (her name is Marzia) that there had been someone able to manage the situation in that way.

E.G. – Rocca di Papa (Rome)

We Can Move Mountains

Liverpool, 17 November 1965

We have arrived in Liverpool. During the meeting for Anglicans to be held tonight, the bishop has insisted that only three Catholics should be present. We've reached this point!

Later

This morning we drove through Liverpool. There are two cathedrals, one Anglican, which is already built; the other, Catholic, which is under construction. They are linked by Hope Street.

The Gospel for today said that if we have faith, we can move mountains.' We have asked that the mountain of mutual incomprehension between the two Churches be moved.

And that's how it was this evening: one of those uncomplicated but decisive meetings. I think that only God will know how important it was.

6 May 2002

In Great Britain today, there are eight focolares, in various places such as London, Liverpool, Leeds and Edinburgh. One is made up of Anglicans, and the others of Catholics and Anglicans. There is a little town of ecumenical witness at Welwyn Garden City, near London, a publishing house, New City, and thousands of people of various Churches who live the 'dialogue of life', sharing the spirituality of unity with us in various ways. With faith mountains can be moved.

From Chiara's diary

Chiara Lubich and the Focolare Movement: A Brief History

The Beginning

Chiara Lubich was born in Trent on 22 January 1920, the second of four children. Her mother was a fervent Catholic, her father a socialist.

When she was just over twenty years old, she taught in a primary school and began studying philosophy at Venice University, drawn by a passion to search for the truth. During the Second World War, when everything collapsed, she understood that only God remains. She made God-Love (cf. 1 Jn 4:8) the ideal of her life, choosing him as her 'all'. The day was 7 December 1943, and this date is taken to mark the beginning of the Movement.

On 13 May 1944 Trent was struck by one of the most violent bombing raids. The Lubich house was also hit. While her family fled to the mountains, Chiara decided to stay in Trent so as not to abandon this new life, which was just beginning.

In the chaos she embraced a woman who, sent mad by her suffering, was crying out loud. She had lost four of her relatives. Chiara became aware of the call to embrace humanity's sufferings. After a short while she found an apartment, which she shared with her first companions.

When they went into the air-raid shelters all they took with them was a copy of the New Testament. Its words seemed lit up with a new light and Chiara and her companions felt compelled to translate them into life immediately.

It was among the poor of Trent that Chiara began what she calls 'a divine adventure': 'As you did it to one of the least of these members of my family, you did it to me.' (Mt 25:40). They shared all that they had with the poor. Even in the throes of war, food, clothing and medicine came with unusual abundance, for their many needs. They experienced the realization of the evangelical promises: 'Give, and it will be given to you' (Lk 6:38), 'Ask, and it will be given to you' (Lk 11:9). From this they were convinced that the Gospel lived out is the solution to every personal and social problem.

In the words of Jesus, translated one by one into daily life, and in particular in the commandment that Jesus calls 'new' and his own, 'Love one another as I have loved you,' (Jn 15:12), they intuited that there was the law by which humanity, which was disintegrating, could be made whole on the model of the Trinity. They saw the measure of this love in the climax of Jesus' suffering on the cross, when he gave his life and reached the point of crying out: 'My God, my God, why have you forsaken me?' (Mt 27:46).

They experienced joy, peace, strength, the fruits of the Holy Spirit, because of the presence of the Risen Lord, as promised by him to 'two or three gathered together in his name' (cf. Mt 18:20), that is, in his love. And in Jesus' testament: 'May they all be one'

(Jn 17:21), they found the reason for their life: 'We were born for unity, to contribute to its realization in the world'.

A number of manual workers and professionals, attracted by the radicality of the Gospel as lived by that first group, joined them. Soon so did families, people of all types and ages, priests and religious. After a few months there were about five hundred taking part in a spontaneous communion of all they had, both material and spiritual. It was community modelled on the style of the early Christians who 'were of one heart and soul, and ... they had everything in common.' (At. 4:32). Carlo De Ferrari, their bishop, affirmed, 'Here is the hand of God.' And he gave his first approval.

Spread and Development

A current of spirituality grew up on the basis of living the Gospel. It was a spirituality of unity. This distinctly communitarian way came to be recognized by the Roman Catholic Church, and also by other Churches, as the result of a charism sent by Holy Spirit to reawaken the life of the Gospel in the world today.

From that small group began a movement of spiritual and social renewal. It came to be called the Focolare Movement.

Over the years it has developed into something like a people in miniature spread throughout the world. By the year 2000 it existed in more than a hundred and eighty countries, with more than five million adherents, belonging not only to the Roman Catholic Church but also to three hundred and fifty other Christian denominations. Little by little some of the faithful of other religions and people who do not have any religious convictions have become involved in a unique project: to live and spread universal brotherhood and so contribute to uniting the human family, especially where there is conflict and division.

As Chiara herself affirms, the Movement is 'in continual development and was not thought up by any human mind, but comes from on high. We try to follow his will day by day.'[23]

From her meeting in 1948 with Igino Giordani, a Member of the Italian Parliament, writer, ecumenist and father of four children, the growing Movement opened up to society, the family and to the ecumenical world. Giordani's influence was so important that he came to be considered a co-founder of the Movement. Through meeting people who had fled from Communist Europe, the Movement discovered the suffering Church behind the Iron Curtain. This led, from the 1960s, to the spirituality of unity spreading throughout Eastern Europe.

Influence of the Charism of Unity

The Movement creates 'pieces of brotherhood' everywhere, in the first place through dialogue with members of the same Church, then among Christians of different traditions, then with the faithful of various religions, then with people without any specifically religious convictions and, finally, through involvement in different sectors of society. Brotherhood is possible

---

23. Cf. Talk to the Catholic University of Lubjiana, 1996 in *Nuova umanitá*, No. 105/106, pp. 313–326.

because, as Chiara has often affirmed, 'We have all been created in the image and likeness of God, who is Love. The law of loving is written into the DNA of every person.'[24]

Christians from all Churches, most of whom have in common the fundamental elements of baptism, Holy Scripture, the Creed, and the early councils, as well as sharing in the common spirituality of unity, join with the Roman Catholics of the Movement in forming a dialogue 'of the people'. What develops is so powerful that it can be thought of as a single Christian soul animating the one Church, which is the aim and the fruit of ecumenism.

Inter-religious dialogue developed as a result of the interest shown by Jews, Muslims and Hindus in London in 1977, when Chiara told her experience in the Guildhall during the ceremony in which she received the Templeton Prize for progress in religion. She was subsequently invited to bring her spiritual experience to Buddhist temples, as in Tokyo at the beginning of 1980, and fifteen years later in Thailand. This invitation has been extended by others. At the end of the 1990s it led Chiara to speak at the Malcolm X Mosque in Harlem, New York. This stimulated interest in the Focolare's spirituality in forty Mosques in various cities in the United States, to say nothing of the Jewish centres. The relationship of brotherhood that developed was particularly valuable after the attack on the Twin Towers on 11 September 2001.

---

24. From the Talk to the International Congress of the Parochial and Diocesan Movement 'For a community in dialogue', Castelgandolfo (Rome), 20 April 2002.

And finally, there is dialogue with people of other, non-religious convictions. In this all work together for the protection of human values.

The Movement's social impact can be seen as a result of the Gospel experience of 'Give, and it will be given to you' lived in the Focolare's early days. It has been repeated over the years in the most diverse of daily situations through the communion of goods that has become a way of life in the Movement. This has led to more than a thousand projects and activities of a social nature. In developing countries, people in need find a way of emerging from sub-human situations.

During a journey to Brazil in 1991, Chiara was struck by the drama of economic destitution on the outskirts of a metropolis such as Saõ Paolo. This led her to launch the Economy of Communion project. Now it inspires the way in which hundreds of small businesses in the world are run and makes it possible to foresee the development of a new economic theory.

The political crises, which affected Italy and other countries, halfway through the nineties, gave rise to the Movement for Unity, which has brotherhood as its fundamental political value.

The activity of people of all walks of life means that the Gospel penetrates not just the worlds of economy, work and politics, but also the worlds of law, philosophy, education, art, social communication, science, health and ecology. Here too these various spheres are reformed according to the values of communion and solidarity.

This is a contribution to a 'globalization' of solidarity and communion that serves as an antidote to economic globalization's increasing social and cultural inequality.

In the Abba School Chiara with a number of academics is developing a new set of ideas that grow out of the humus of the spirituality. It casts light on a wide range of disciplines. This creative development has been recognized by universities in many parts of the world and numerous honorary degrees have been conferred on Chiara.

'The development of the Focolare Movement builds bridges between persons, generations, social classes and peoples, in an age in which ethnic and religious differences lead all too often to violent conflict.' This was in the citation for the 1996 UNESCO Prize for Peace Education. The same thing has been recognized by other international prizes, such as the 1998 Prize for Human Rights, and the honorary citizenships conferred on Chiara by cities such as Buenos Aires, Florence and Rome.

In these times, in which women seek the role in society and in the Church that belongs to them, Chiara Lubich demonstrates with her life what is specific to women: the charism of love which creates unity. The Focolare Movement's statutes, confirmed by the Roman Catholic Church, state that, even with all the diversity of the vocations within it, the Movement will always have a laywoman as its President.